# THE HAIRY BIKERS'
# VEGGIE FEASTS

Si King & Dave Myers

# THE HAIRY BIKERS'

# VEGGIE FEASTS

# CONTENTS

Brunch 12

Salads 32

Soups 60

Snacks & light dishes 86

Easy meals 120

Weekend specials 160

Puddings & bakes 210

Sides & basics 246

Index 278

# GREAT FOOD, GREAT FLAVOUR

**You know us – we love food that's hearty, satisfying and that tastes amazing. That's what we do. For this book, we've created a new collection of superb recipes that you'll love cooking, eating and serving to your friends and family. Great taste is the bottom line as always, but these dishes happen to be vegetarian and/or vegan as well, so we reckon it's a win win!**

This is a book we've wanted to write for a long time, and we've approached these dishes from the point of view of meat eaters, aiming to pack the food with flavour, colour and texture in such a way that you really don't miss meat. The recipes are a culmination of many years of enjoying and experimenting with different types of food from all over the world, and we believe they reflect the way we all want to eat now. There are great fry-ups, beautiful soups, an incredible Indian curry version of shepherd's pie, veggie sausages, a vegan BLT, pickled onion bhajis, mushroom mini kievs, tacos, pizzas and the perfect veggie burger to name just a few. Even our salads are satisfying complete meals – there's something here for everyone.

When we were growing up, a meal wasn't a meal without some meat – or perhaps a bit of fish. But things have changed big time. Even before we wrote our *Hairy Dieters Go Veggie* book back in 2017, we'd found we were eating less and less meat. On some of our travels while filming we've been to countries where eating mostly plant-based food was part of the culture, and we were really happy with that.

We realised that while we might not go totally vegetarian, we enjoyed cooking and eating plant-based meals and that they tasted really good. The other thing that happened – and we know this is the case with many families – was that some of our children decided to go vegetarian or vegan. When they're with us we cook veggie food – and, without wishing to blow our own trumpets, we reckon we've got better and better at it.

Plant-based eating is now hugely popular. More and more people are deciding to go veggie or vegan. Plant-based restaurants are springing up all over the place and regular shops are stocking big ranges of vegetarian and vegan products. No longer do you have to search out these things in special health food stores. It's all readily available in the supermarkets.

What's more, growing your own veg has never been so popular. There are long waiting lists for allotments, people are planting vegetables in their garden and growing herbs on balconies and windowsills. There's always something you can plant whatever space you have. There's nothing like plucking a beautiful ripe tomato from the plant, still warm from the sun, and using it in a wonderful dish like our fab tomato and burrata salad on page 56. We are both loving growing our own these days, and Dave has been particularly proud of his tomato crop this year – 15 different varieties! – and he has also grown padron peppers for the first time. Si, meanwhile, has been nurturing a pick-your-own salad bar in boxes outside his kitchen.

Eating plant-based meals at least some of the time is good for your health, reducing the risk of certain cancers and heart disease and also helping with other problems such as high blood pressure. We find we lose weight too, when we eat veggie. We still have some meat and fish, but not as much as we used to. And when we do, we make sure the meat is properly reared and the fish is from sustainable sources. You might have to pay a bit more but then you're not buying it every day. Shopping and eating this way is also important for the health of the planet and that is something that concerns us all.

For inspiration, we've looked at the food of other parts of the world, such as the Mediterranean, Middle East and India, where much of the diet is naturally plant-based. They use pulses, herbs and spices to enhance meals and manage to pack in so much flavour you don't even think about whether it is vegetarian or not. And that's our modern take on vegetarian cooking too – light years away from the brown stodge served up in the early days of veggie restaurants in the 80s. We've concentrated on using good fresh ingredients, and we avoid processed products as much as possible.

When we first started to think about this book the ideas flowed like lava. We got so excited and we ended up with more than twice as many recipes as we could possibly fit in. Sometimes we just couldn't make up our minds which way to go, so we got on to Instagram and asked you guys! Hope you like the results. Whether you want to go full-on veggie or vegan or just to eat more delicious plant-based meals, we think you'll find plenty to enjoy in this book. We're really chuffed with these recipes and we hope you are too. So get cooking!

# VITAMINS AND MINERALS

Vegetables and fruit are packed with nutrients, so a plant-based diet is really healthy. For proof of this, just look at the Blue Zones – places in the world where a much larger percentage of the population than average lives to over a hundred. We went to some of the Sardinian Blue Zone villages, where the diet is based on veg and fruit, wholegrains and a small amount of meat – and the food we ate was delicious. If you do opt to go totally vegan, check you are getting all the vitamins and minerals you need. There's plenty of advice on the Vegan Society website.

| | |
|---|---|
| Vitamin A | Sweet potatoes, carrots, peppers, tomatoes, broccoli and other green leafy veg, tomatoes, spinach, squash, asparagus, peas, lettuce, apricots, peaches, plums. |
| Vitamin B | Broccoli, spinach, asparagus, potatoes, bananas, nuts; dried fruit, such as apricots, dates and figs. |
| Vitamin C | Broccoli, spinach, kale, Brussels sprouts, cabbage, cauliflower, peppers, potatoes, peas, oranges, strawberries, raspberries. |
| Vitamin E | Avocados, tomatoes, sweet potatoes, spinach, watercress, nuts and seeds, blackberries, mangoes. |
| Calcium | Green leafy veg, such as kale, watercress and broccoli; okra, pulses, dried figs and apricots, almonds. |
| Iron | Spinach, kale, watercress, broccoli, cabbage and other dark green leafy veg; beans and lentils, dried fruit. |
| Potassium | Potatoes, bananas and other fresh fruit; dried fruit, such as prunes. |
| Zinc | Nuts and seeds, pulses, fresh peas, watercress, spinach, asparagus, dried fruit. |

# NOTES FROM US

• Peel onions, garlic and other veg and fruit unless otherwise specified.

• Weigh all your ingredients and use proper measuring spoons. We've made the oven temperatures as accurate as possible, but all ovens are different so keep an eye on your dish and be prepared to cook it for a longer or shorter time if necessary.

• Use free-range eggs whenever possible. And we generally use large eggs in our recipes unless otherwise specified.

• Check that any wine or sherry you use is vegan/vegetarian friendly. Some do include animal proteins.

• Be careful about cheese. Many cheeses are made with animal rennet, but you can find plenty of good cheese that is suitable for vegetarians. Check the labels when buying, and you'll also find lots of helpful advice on the Vegetarian Society website. There are some vegan cheeses now.

• As you know, going vegan means not eating any animal-based products at all, so no cheese, no eggs, no butter, no honey. We've aimed to make around 30 per cent of the recipes in this book vegan and there are more that can be adapted to a vegan diet with small changes, such as using a plant-based milk instead of cow's milk or leaving out cheese. We've added tips on all of that.

• There's a wide range of unsweetened plant-based milk now, including oat, rice and almond as well as soya, and you can use all of these as substitutes for cow's milk.

• Home-made stock is great to have in your freezer, so we've included a couple of stock recipes at the back of the book. Some dishes, such as risotto, really do benefit hugely from a good stock. But if you don't have time, there are good fresh stocks available in the supermarkets or you can use the little stock pots or cubes.

All recipes are veggie Ⓥ, many are vegan Ⓥ, and look out for *BIKER VEGAN TIPS* and notes in the recipes for easy ways to adapt more recipes for vegans.

Masala frittata 16

Chickpea pancakes with spicy carrot & bean curry 18

Tofu scramble fry-up 20

Tomato & olive French toast 22

Tattie scones 24

Farmhouse hash 26

Indian bubble & squeak 28

American-style pancakes 30

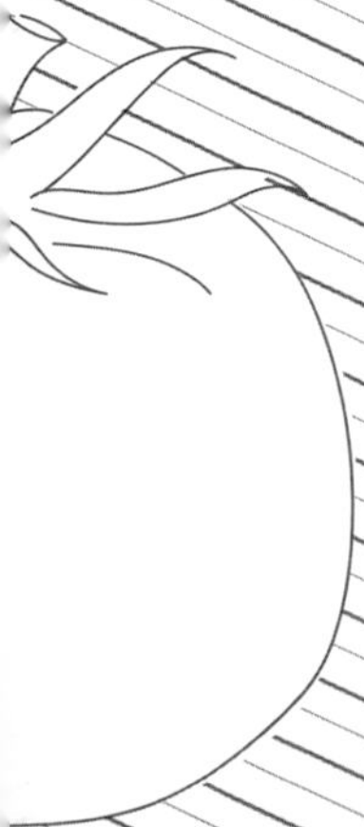

2 tbsp olive oil

2 onions, sliced

200g cooked salad potatoes, diced

200g blanched cauliflower,
  cut into fairly small florets

1 garlic clove, finely chopped

1 tsp nigella seeds

1 tsp cumin seeds

1 tsp ground turmeric

½ tsp chilli powder

100g mature vegetarian Cheddar
  or similar, grated

6 eggs, beaten

2 green chillies, very finely sliced

sea salt and black pepper

**Coriander yoghurt sauce**

100g plain or coconut yoghurt

small bunch of coriander,
  very finely chopped

juice of 1 lime

1 tsp light soft brown sugar
  or jaggery

# Masala frittata

**We've gone full-on fusion with no confusion here, taking an Italian omelette or frittata and adding loads of great Indian flavour, plus some good old British Cheddar cheese. Might sound a bit crazy, but it's a really good eat and gets you going in the morning. Nice served with some roasted cherry tomatoes on the side. Try this – it works.**

Heat the olive oil in an ovenproof, non-stick (or cast-iron) frying pan. Add the onions and cook for about 10 minutes over a medium heat until they are soft and have taken on lots of colour. Add the potatoes and cauliflower, leave to cook for 3–4 minutes, then stir. Cook for another few minutes until the potatoes and cauliflower have crisped up and browned in places.

Add the garlic and sprinkle in the nigella and cumin seeds. Add the turmeric and chilli powder and stir to combine, then sprinkle over the cheese. Season the eggs with plenty of salt and pepper, then pour them over the vegetables as evenly as you can.

Preheat the grill to a medium heat. Cook the frittata for several minutes on the hob over a medium heat until the base is cooked through but the top is still slightly soft. Sprinkle over the green chillies and put the pan under the grill until the frittata is lightly browned and puffed up.

For the sauce, blend the yoghurt with the coriander, lime juice and sugar or jaggery. Season with plenty of salt. Serve the frittata cut into wedges, with the sauce on the side.

# Chickpea pancakes with spicy carrot & bean curry

**Chickpea pancakes**

150g gram (chickpea) flour

1 tbsp olive oil, plus extra for frying

4 tbsp finely chopped coriander

**Spicy carrots and beans**

2 tbsp coconut oil

½ tsp ground turmeric

¼ tsp ground cinnamon

25g fresh root ginger, grated

200g carrots, grated

200g white or green pointed cabbage, finely shredded

100g green beans, sliced into rounds

75g fresh coconut, grated or processed

½ tsp mustard seeds

a few curry leaves

sea salt and black pepper

**To serve (optional)**

plant-based coconut yoghurt

Curry for breakfast? Yes! We became addicted to the idea of starting the day the spicy way when we spent time filming in southern India. This is a version of the dry vegetable curry known as thoran, which comes from Kerala. The veg can be varied but the curry always contains coconut. We think it goes beautifully with these chickpea flour pancakes to make a really special brunch dish.

To make the pancakes, whisk the gram flour with 300ml of water, the oil and the coriander. Leave to stand for half an hour.

Meanwhile, prepare the vegetables. Heat a tablespoon of the coconut oil in a large frying pan and add the spices and ginger. Fry for a minute or so, then add the carrots, cabbage and beans. Season with salt and pepper, then continue to fry, stirring regularly, until the vegetables have collapsed down and the beans are just tender. Stir in the coconut with 50ml of water and continue to cook for a few more minutes over a very low heat. Set aside and keep warm.

When you are ready to cook the pancakes, heat a crêpe pan (ideally one with a base of about 18cm) over a high heat and add a little olive oil. Ladle over some of the batter and swirl it round to cover the base of the pan. Let it set, then gradually loosen it around the sides and flip – the pancake should have a pockmarked texture and be slightly crisp. Cook on the other side, then remove and set aside. Repeat until you have used all the batter, adding a little more oil each time. You should get about 8 pancakes.

To finish the thoran, heat the remaining tablespoon of coconut oil in a separate pan and add the mustard seeds and curry leaves. When the curry leaves crackle and are very aromatic, remove the pan from the heat and pour the mixture over the vegetables. Serve with the pancakes and perhaps some coconut yoghurt.

# Tofu scramble fry-up

**Tofu scramble**

1 x 280–300g block of extra-firm tofu

2 tbsp olive oil

4 spring onions, finely sliced

2 garlic cloves, finely chopped

½ tsp dried oregano

½ tsp garlic powder

¼ tsp ground turmeric

1 tbsp tamari

large sprig of tarragon, finely chopped

100g baby leaf spinach (optional)

sea salt and black pepper

**Fried tomatoes and mushrooms**

3 tbsp olive oil

4 medium/large tomatoes, halved

8 chestnut or field mushrooms, halved

leaves from a sprig of thyme

**Fried slice**

extra olive oil as necessary

4 slices of bread

**To serve**

tofu bacon (see p.266)

home-made baked beans (see p.253)

Everyone loves a good fry-up and if you're vegan, there's no reason why you can't still enjoy all those great flavours. We've given you the whole vegan version of a full English for when you feel like a real slap-up feast, but you could just choose the bits you fancy. Don't miss out the fried slice though!

First, press the tofu – this will help expel excess liquid and improve the flavour and texture. Place the tofu between 2 plates, weigh it down with a couple of tins and leave it to stand for about an hour, straining off the liquid at regular intervals.

When you're ready to cook, heat the oil in a large frying pan. Add the spring onions, garlic, oregano, garlic powder and turmeric, then fry for a few minutes until the spring onions have started to soften. Crumble in the tofu together with the tamari and tarragon and season with salt and pepper. Continue to cook, stirring very regularly, until the tofu has absorbed some colour from the spices and tamari and is cooked through. If using the spinach, wash it well, then wilt it down in a separate pan and strain. Stir it through the tofu until piping hot.

For the mushrooms and tomatoes, heat the oil in another large frying pan. Sprinkle the tomatoes with salt, then arrange them, cut-side down, on one side of the frying pan. Leave to cook over a high heat for 2 minutes, until they look as though they are caramelising round the edges, then turn them over and cook on the skin side for another 2–3 minutes until cooked through but still holding their shape.

While the tomatoes are cooking, sprinkle the mushrooms with some salt and add them to the other side of the pan. Add the thyme leaves and fry, turning regularly, until lightly browned.

Remove the tomatoes and mushrooms from the pan and set aside. Add a little more oil if necessary, then add the slices of bread. Fry until the underside is crisp and glossy, then flip over – if the pan looks very dry, add more olive oil. Serve with the tofu scramble and some tofu bacon and baked beans.

**Tomato & olive bread**

500g strong white bread flour, plus extra for dusting

7g instant yeast (1 sachet)

2 tsp sugar

1 tsp salt

150ml tomato juice, at room temperature

100g sunblush tomatoes, at room temperature

2 tbsp olive oil

100g green olives (pitted weight), sliced

**Mozzarella French toast**

400g vegetarian mozzarella, grated

8 slices of tomato and olive bread

a few basil leaves

3 eggs

80ml milk

½ tsp dried oregano

olive oil, for frying

sea salt and black pepper

# Tomato & olive French toast

We've been experimenting with flavoured breads and we're really happy with this Mediterranean-inspired tomato and olive version. Then we came up with the idea of using it to make French toast mozzarella sandwiches – genius or what? The mozzarella you buy in blocks is best here, as it's firmer and easier to grate.

To make the bread dough, put the flour in a bowl (or a stand mixer) with the yeast and sugar. Stir thoroughly, then add the salt and stir again. Do not add the yeast and salt together without mixing – if the salt comes into contact with the yeast it will inhibit its action.

Purée the tomato juice and tomatoes together until smooth. Add enough just-boiled water to bring their combined weight up to 325g. Add the oil to the flour, then gradually work in the tomato mixture. Mix until you have a smooth dough, then leave the dough to stand for half an hour.

Add the olives, knead them in and continue to knead until the dough is soft and pliable. This will take about 5 minutes in a stand mixer or 10 minutes by hand. To judge whether the dough is ready, take a section and stretch it out as much as you can in all directions. If you can stretch the dough so thin that you can almost see through it, it's been kneaded enough.

Cover the dough with a damp cloth and leave it somewhere warm to rise until it has doubled in size. This will take at least an hour, longer depending on the temperature. Preheat the oven to 220°C/Fan 200°C/Gas 7.

Turn out the dough and knock it back, then give it another quick knead and shape it into an oval loaf. Place it on a floured baking tray, cover again and leave for at least half an hour until it has risen into a smooth dome. Bake for about 25 minutes, until it is well risen, deep brown and sounds hollow when you knock on the base. Leave to cool completely.

To make French toast, divide the mozzarella between 4 slices of the bread and scatter over a few basil leaves. Top with the remaining slices of bread and squash each sandwich together around the edges.

Whisk the eggs and milk together in a bowl and add the oregano and plenty of seasoning. Dip both sides of each sandwich into the mixture and let any excess drip off. There is no need to immerse the sandwiches completely, just make sure the outsides are completely coated.

Heat the oil in a large frying pan and fry the sandwiches for 3–4 minutes on each side until they are crisp and well browned. Don't worry if some mozzarella escapes – it will crisp up nicely in the pan. Cut in half and serve piping hot with a good dollop of ketchup or some tomato relish (see p.259).

500g floury potatoes (such as Maris Pipers), unpeeled and cut into large chunks

150–175g plain flour, plus extra for dusting

1 tsp baking powder

1 egg, beaten

50g butter, plus extra for frying

sea salt and black pepper

**To serve (optional)**

fermented tomatoes (see p. 260)

# Tattie scones

**A classic treat that never goes out of fashion. Slathered with butter and served with fermented tomatoes, these potato scones are so good. They're great with a bit of Marmite too, or you can go the sweet route and dish them up with jam or honey. We like to steam the potatoes as described below to get them as dry as possible, then mix them into the flour while still hot. This gives you lighter, more tender scones.**

Put the potatoes in a steamer basket over a pan of boiling water and steam them for about 20 minutes until completely tender. Remove from the heat and, while the potatoes are still hot, peel off the skins. Wear rubber gloves for this or spear each piece of potato with a fork and peel the skin off with a sharp knife – they should slide off easily.

Put 150g of the flour and the baking powder into a bowl with plenty of salt and pepper. Mash the still-hot potatoes straight into the flour – the best way to do this is to put the potatoes through a ricer, holding it over the bowl of flour. Add the egg and the 50g of butter – the butter should melt into the potato. Mix until you have a soft dough. If it seems too soft and doesn't hold together, add a little more of the flour.

Knead the mixture briefly until it is smooth, then turn it out on to a generously floured surface. Cut the dough into 6 equal pieces, then roll each piece into a round of about 12–15cm in diameter and ½cm thick.

Heat a little butter in a frying pan. Keep the heat at medium – much hotter and the butter will burn and the potato scones will brown too quickly. Fry one round at a time, flipping it over when the underside is brown. It should take 2–3 minutes on each side. Continue until all the rounds are cooked, then cut each round into 4 pieces.

Eat hot, straight out of the pan or reheat by toasting. Serve with butter, fermented tomatoes, if using, and any condiments you like.

# Farmhouse hash

Serves 4

500g floury potatoes (such as Maris Pipers), unpeeled and finely diced

4 tbsp olive oil

200g mushrooms, roughly chopped

½ portion vegan sausages (see p.98), sliced

25g butter

1 large onion, finely chopped

2 tsp mushroom ketchup

½ tsp dried thyme

4 very fresh eggs

1 tsp vinegar

sea salt and black pepper

Our hash recipe is based on one cooked for us by a yodelling instructor called Fritz on a mountain in Austria – all three of us were wearing lederhosen! We didn't improve our yodelling but the hash filled our tummies a treat. We've put this in the brunch chapter, but we believe you can eat hash at any time of day from breakfast to midnight – or later. Use our sausage recipe on page 98 and make sure you steam them first, then leave to cool before frying. This way they will be firm enough to slice nicely.

Put the potatoes in a steamer basket and steam over a pan of simmering water for 10 minutes until almost tender. Meanwhile, heat a tablespoon of the olive oil in a frying pan and fry the mushrooms over a high heat until any liquid has evaporated and they are lightly browned. Remove from the pan and set aside.

Add another tablespoon of oil and fry the sausages on all sides until crisp, then break them up a bit and continue to fry for a few more minutes. Remove from the pan.

Heat the remaining oil in the pan and add the butter. When it is foaming, add the onion and the cooked potatoes and season well with salt and pepper. Cook over a high heat, leaving the mixture for at least 2 or 3 minutes before turning, to get a crisp, brown underside. Continue to cook, turning regularly, until the onion and potatoes are crisp and brown in places – don't stint on this, it should take about 20 minutes. Add the mushroom ketchup and thyme, then put the mushrooms and sausages back in the pan. Continue to cook until everything is piping hot.

To poach the eggs, half-fill a large saucepan with water and add the vinegar. Lower an egg into the water, still uncracked in its shell, and count for 20 seconds. Carefully remove it, crack it into the water and cook for 3 minutes. Repeat with the remaining eggs, draining them on kitchen paper before serving with the hash.

# Indian bubble & squeak

2 tbsp olive oil (or coconut oil)

1 onion, finely chopped

1 tsp ground turmeric

1 tsp ground cumin

1 tsp garam masala

2–3 green chillies, finely chopped

400g cooked potatoes, unpeeled, roughly crushed

250g cooked greens (cabbage, kale, chard, spring greens, broccoli)

sea salt and black pepper

**To serve**

mango chutney

Everyone loves a good old bubble and squeak but adding Indian spices really makes it a breakfast of champions. This is a great reboot of the traditional recipe and perks you up a treat. It's a cracking way to use up any leftover veg too – and it's so tasty it's worth cooking the vegetables specially! Use any greens you have available.

Heat the oil in a non-stick or cast-iron frying pan. Add the onion and cook over a medium heat until it has softened and is lightly caramelised.

Add the turmeric, cumin, garam masala and chillies, and season with salt and pepper. Stir to coat the onions, then add the potatoes and greens. Stir again, so everything takes on a yellow hue from the turmeric, then press it all down.

Leave to cook over a medium heat for 5 minutes, then stir, making sure you scrape up all the brown bits from the base of the pan. Press down again and continue to cook in this way, mixing it all up every few minutes until you are happy you have enough brown bits flecked through the potatoes.

Serve with some mango chutney.

200g plain flour
(or spelt or wholemeal)

2 tsp baking powder

½ tsp bicarbonate of soda

½ tsp ground cinnamon

1 tsp mixed spice

2 tbsp caster sugar

pinch of salt

300ml plant-based milk
(soya or almond)

1 tbsp apple cider vinegar
or lemon juice

coconut oil

**To serve**

maple syrup

fresh berries

# American-style pancakes

Both of us like plant-based milk. It's a great thing to have in the store cupboard and it really does make light fluffy pancakes. A generous pile of American pancakes is one of our favourite breakfasts and it's great to have a vegan version. Just make sure the pan you have is completely non-stick, or use a really well-seasoned cast-iron pan. Take care when cooking the pancakes, and don't flip them too soon or they may crack.

Mix the flour with the baking powder, bicarbonate of soda, spices and sugar in a large bowl. Stir in a generous pinch of salt. Mix the milk with the vinegar and stir – it should thicken slightly. (By the way, oat milk doesn't thicken properly when you add vinegar, so stick with soya or almond milk.) Pour the wet ingredients into the dry and combine, but try to keep mixing to a minimum.

Heat a tablespoon of coconut oil in a non-stick frying pan or a cast-iron pan, pour it into the batter and stir.

Add more coconut oil to the pan. Keep the heat at medium to high and spoon 4 small ladlefuls of batter on to the pan, making sure they are well spaced apart. When they look set around the edges and large bubbles have appeared, carefully flip one of them over. If it is a deep brown, flip the rest and cook on the reverse side for another minute. Remove and set aside while you cook the rest of the pancakes in the same way.

Continue until you have used up all the batter, adding a little more oil to the pan each time. Serve with plenty of maple syrup and some fresh berries.

Roast beetroot, goat's cheese & apple salad 36

Mexican buddha bowl 38

Broad bean, radish & potato salad 40

Green bean, orange & hazelnut salad 42

Bean, marinated tofu & broccoli salad 44

Noodle salad with greens & mushrooms 46

Greek salad with roast tomatoes & halloumi 48

Grilled vegetable & freekeh salad 50

Thai-spiced mushroom salad 52

Asparagus mimosa 54

Tomato & burrata salad 56

American-style layered salad 58

# Roast beetroot, goat's cheese & apple salad

6 smallish beetroots

1 tbsp olive oil

sprigs of thyme

100g watercress, broken into small sprigs

about 50g lamb's lettuce or other salad greens

1 or 2 crisp eating apples, cored and diced

about 150g vegetarian goat's cheese log, thinly sliced

small bunch of parsley, torn into small sprigs

30g walnuts, roughly chopped

sea salt and black pepper

**Dressing**

1 shallot, finely sliced

leaves from a sprig of thyme

1 tbsp cider vinegar

3 tbsp walnut or olive oil

Roasting beetroot is dead simple and gives a better texture and flavour to this tasty salad but if you're short of time, it's fine to use the vacuum-packed beets you can buy in the supermarket. If you have the fresh stuff, you can add the beet leaves to the salad or cook them in the same way as you would kale or chard. We like leaving the apples unpeeled for an extra bit of colour and texture. A great salad.

If you're using fresh raw beetroot, preheat the oven to 200°C/ Fan 180°C/Gas 6. Cut the stems off the beetroot about 1cm from the top – leaving this little bit of stem stops the beetroot 'bleeding' as it cooks. Wash and dry the beetroots thoroughly, then put them in a roasting tin and drizzle over the oil. Add plenty of thyme and season with salt and pepper. Cover the tin with foil and roast the beetroots for 40–50 minutes, depending on their size. They're ready once they are tender all the way through.

Leave the beets to cool for a few minutes until cool enough to handle, then rub off the skins. Set aside to cool, then dice. If using vacuum-packed beetroot, just dice them.

For the salad dressing, add the shallot and thyme leaves to the cider vinegar and leave to stand for 10 minutes. Season with salt and plenty of pepper, then whisk in the oil.

Assemble the salad on a large serving platter or in 4 individual bowls. Lightly toss the watercress and other salad leaves with the apple and beetroot. Top with the slices of goat's cheese and add the parsley sprigs and walnuts. Drizzle over the salad dressing and serve immediately with some crusty bread if you like.

# Mexican buddha bowl

**Lime-pickled red onion**

juice of 2 limes

1 tsp salt

1 red onion, finely sliced

**Tomato salsa**

100g tomatoes, finely chopped

1 red pepper, deseeded and
    finely chopped

1 garlic clove, finely chopped

small bunch of coriander,
    finely chopped

zest and juice of 1 lime

1 tsp red wine vinegar

1 or 2 fresh jalapeños or similar,
    finely chopped

sea salt and black pepper

**Roasted sweetcorn**

2 tsp coconut oil or olive oil

300g sweetcorn, fresh or frozen

½ tsp chipotle or smoked chilli
    powder

**Black beans**

1 tsp coconut oil or olive oil

½ tsp ground cinnamon

½ tsp ground cumin

1 tsp dried oregano

500g cooked black beans (see p.274)
    or 2 cans of beans, drained

**To assemble**

1 large cos lettuce, shredded

300g cooked quinoa (see p.271)

2 avocados, peeled, and sliced
    lengthways

juice of 1 lime

vegan cream sauce
    (see p.262 – optional)

coriander sprigs

There's loads of great flavours and textures in this recipe – a real rainbow feast of a dish – and if you like you can add a nice vegan cream sauce (see page 262). If you're not vegan you could just use soured cream, thinned down with a little lime juice. You'll find advice on cooking quinoa on page 271 and black beans on page 274, but it's fine to use canned beans and ready-cooked quinoa if you prefer. It's cheaper to cook your own though!

First make the pickled red onion. Put the lime juice in a bowl with the salt. In a separate bowl, pour boiling water over the red onion and leave to stand for 20 seconds, then drain and add to the bowl of lime juice. Toss gently until all the onion is covered in juice, then leave to stand for about half an hour until the onion turns bright pink. Set aside.

To make the tomato salsa, mix all the ingredients together and season with plenty of salt and pepper.

For the roasted sweetcorn, heat the oil in a frying pan and add the sweetcorn – you can cook it from frozen if you like. Fry over a medium to high heat, stirring regularly, until the sweetcorn is well browned in places. Sprinkle in the chipotle or smoked chilli powder and add plenty of salt. Leave to cool.

For the black beans, heat the oil in a frying pan and add the spices and oregano. Fry for a minute to toast lightly, then remove the pan from the heat. Stir in the black beans to coat them and set aside.

To assemble, divide the lettuce between 4 bowls. Arrange portions of quinoa, tomato salsa, sweetcorn and black beans around the sides. Toss the avocado in the lime juice and add this as well. Spoon a little of the vegan cream sauce in the middle of the bowl, if using, then drain the lime-pickled onions and add these on top. Garnish with a few coriander sprigs.

SERVES 4

200g broad beans (podded weight)
500g small new/salad potatoes,
    washed or scraped and
    sliced if large
200g radishes, preferably with leaves
100g salad leaves, such as rocket
    or spinach
sea salt and black pepper

**Dressing**
small bunch of dill
2 tbsp crème fraiche
1 tbsp olive oil
zest of 1 lemon
juice of ½ lemon
1 tsp wholegrain mustard
small bunch of dill

# Broad bean, radish & potato salad

**Broad beans and dill work so well together and there's a lovely mix of textures and colours in this summery salad. We both like broad beans but to peel or not to peel – that is the question. Those greyish outer skins can be tough, so we think peeling is worthwhile unless you're using very tiny beans. If you have spanking fresh broad beans, pod them first, obviously.**

First cook the broad beans. Add them to a pan of boiling water and cook for 2 minutes, then drain and refresh under cold water. Peel them, then set the beans aside. With the little frozen ones, the skins pop off easily after blanching.

Cook the potatoes in plenty of boiling, salted water until tender to the point of a knife, then drain and leave to cool.

Wash the radishes thoroughly and slice thinly. If you have radishes with their leaves attached, trim the stems 3–4mm from the top, then add any leaves to the salad greens.

For the dressing, finely chop about 2 tablespoons of the dill leaves, keeping the rest as larger fronds to garnish the salad. Whisk the chopped dill with the remaining ingredients and season with salt and pepper. Pour half the dressing over the potatoes while they are still slightly warm.

To assemble the salad, arrange the salad leaves and radish leaves on a serving dish and gently fold in the potatoes, radishes and broad beans. Season with salt and pepper, drizzle over the remaining dressing and garnish with the dill fronds. Serve the salad at room temperature.

 **BIKER VEGAN TIP**

**To make this salad vegan, use a plant-based créme fraiche.**

2 large oranges

250g green beans, trimmed but tails left intact

200g cooked lentils

75g celeriac, cut into matchsticks

100g salad leaves

50g hazelnuts, lightly toasted and roughly chopped

a few fresh oregano leaves

**Dressing**

2 tbsp hazelnut or olive oil

1 tbsp sherry vinegar

zest and juice from the oranges (see method)

1 small garlic clove, crushed

sprig of oregano

sea salt and black pepper

# Green bean, orange & hazelnut salad

**This may sound an unusual combination of ingredients, but they do work very well together. The nice crunchiness of the celeriac and nuts combines beautifully with the fresh green beans and salad leaves, while the lentils add protein and texture. The orange slices and citrussy dressing make the perfect finishing touch. A winner, we think.**

First prepare the oranges. Zest half of one of the oranges with a microplane or similar and put the zest in a bowl. Cut away the top and bottom of the orange, then following the contour of the fruit, cut away all the skin, pith and membrane, exposing the orange flesh beneath. Cut the flesh into rounds, flicking out any seeds as you go. If the rounds are particularly large, cut them into half circles. Add any juice from the chopping board to the zest, then squeeze out any juice from the peel – you'll get a surprising amount. Prepare the other orange in the same way.

Make the dressing by adding the oil and vinegar to the orange juice and zest, along with the garlic and plenty of seasoning. Add the oregano – a quick bashing with a pestle or a wooden spoon will leave the sprig whole but will release its flavour and aroma into the dressing. Leave to stand.

Bring a pan of water to the boil and add the beans. Cook for 2 minutes, then refresh the beans in a bowl of iced water or run them under a cold tap.

To assemble the salad, dress the lentils and celeriac with half the dressing and leave to stand for a few minutes. Arrange the salad leaves on a platter or in a large shallow bowl, then add the lentils, celeriac, green beans and orange slices and toss gently. Top with the hazelnuts and oregano, drizzle over the remaining dressing and serve immediately.

# Bean, marinated tofu & broccoli salad

Edamame beans are actually young fresh soybeans and you can buy them in the supermarket in their pods or podded. They are good in this salad, which can be served warm or cold so is perfect for a packed lunch. Tofu is a great flavour carrier and the marinade in this recipe dresses it up for the party.

**Marinade**

2 tbsp miso paste

2 tbsp soy sauce

1 tbsp rice wine vinegar

25g fresh root ginger, grated

salt (optional)

**Salad**

1 x 280–300g block of extra-firm tofu, pressed if necessary (see p.20), cut into 2cm cubes

1 tbsp vegetable oil

300g sprouting or tenderstem broccoli, trimmed

200g cooked brown rice

a few drops of sesame oil

small bag of salad leaves (preferably including mizuna – a Japanese salad leaf)

150g podded edamame/soybeans (about 300g unpodded weight)

small bunch of mint leaves

**Dressing**

juice of ½ lemon

1 tbsp light soy sauce

1 tsp sesame oil

First make the marinade. Whisk all the ingredients together and taste. Add salt if you like. Add the tofu and carefully turn it over in the marinade until completely coated. Leave for at least half an hour – it's fine to leave it overnight.

To make the salad, heat the oil in a frying pan. Strain the tofu, reserving the marinade, and add the tofu to the pan. Fry on all sides until golden brown, then remove from the heat.

Blanch the broccoli in boiling salted water until tender, then drain and refresh in a bowl of iced water or run it under a cold tap. Drain again and set aside.

Dress the brown rice with a few drops of sesame oil. Make the dressing by whisking the lemon juice, soy sauce and sesame oil into the reserved marinade.

Arrange the rice, salad leaves, broccoli, beans and tofu on plates and drizzle over plenty of the dressing. Scatter a few mint leaves over the top, then serve.

# Noodle salad with greens & mushrooms

A Japanese-style salad made with soba noodles, this is a feast of flavours and textures. We had some lovely king oyster mushrooms for our photo, but you can also use enoki or simple button or chestnut. All work well. We've made the coconut optional, as it is a bit of a fiddle to prepare, but it does add a nice touch of sweetness. It must be fresh coconut though, desiccated doesn't work. The pickles in this aren't the preserved sort. They are light and quick to make and really do lift the flavour of the dish.

---

**Turnip and cucumber pickles**

1 large turnip, diced

½ cucumber, peeled, deseeded and sliced into crescents

2 tbsp rice wine vinegar

½ tsp sugar

sea salt

**Salad**

150g soba (buckwheat) noodles

200g greens, such as cavolo nero or kale, leaves stripped from stems and shredded

250g enoki, button, king oyster or chestnut mushrooms, sliced

6 spring onions, finely chopped

20g fresh coconut, peeled and finely sliced (optional)

1 tsp sesame seeds

**Dressing**

1 tbsp sesame oil

2 garlic cloves, finely chopped

15g fresh root ginger, grated

3 tbsp soy sauce

1 tbsp rice vinegar (or more to taste)

1 tbsp rice wine

1 tsp hot sauce (or more to taste)

First make the pickles. Toss the diced turnip and cucumber in the rice wine vinegar, sugar and a teaspoon of salt. Leave to stand while you prepare everything else.

Bring a large saucepan of water to the boil and add the noodles and the greens together. Cook for 3 minutes, then drain and either plunge the noodles and greens into a bowl of iced water or run them under a cold tap until they're cold. Season with a little salt and set aside.

Make the dressing. Heat the oil in a small frying pan over a low heat and add the garlic. Cook gently for a couple of minutes, making sure it doesn't take on any colour, then remove the pan from the heat. Add the ginger and the remaining dressing ingredients and pour into a bowl.

When you are ready to assemble the salad, put the noodles and greens into a bowl. Toss the mushrooms in the dressing very briefly, then add these to the bowl, along with the spring onions. Strain off any liquid from the turnips and cucumber and add these and the coconut, if using. Mix thoroughly and taste – add a little more hot sauce, salt or vinegar if you think it necessary. Divide between 4 bowls and serve sprinkled with sesame seeds.

1–2 tbsp olive oil

200g ripe tomatoes, roughly sliced or chopped

1 tsp dried mint

1 x 225–250g block of halloumi, sliced

sea salt and black pepper

**Salad**

1 large cos or romaine lettuce, roughly torn

½ cucumber, cut into chunks

1 red onion, sliced

1 small green pepper, deseeded and thinly sliced into rounds

1 tbsp olive oil

1 tsp red wine vinegar

50g black olives, pitted if you like

30g capers, rinsed

leaves from a few oregano sprigs

squeeze of lemon juice

# Greek salad with roast tomatoes & halloumi

It's easier to find vegetarian halloumi than feta, so we've gone with halloumi for this recipe and we think it works really well. We both love it anyway – a squeaky cheesy sensation! In a twist on the trad Greek salad, we roast the tomatoes to bring out their flavour and we use the scrumptious juices in the dressing. A summer feast for sure – you'll feel like slathering on the suntan lotion after eating this.

Preheat the oven to 200°C/Fan 180°C/Gas 6. Drizzle a little oil over the base of an ovenproof dish, then add the tomatoes. Drizzle over a little more oil and season with salt and pepper. Place the slices of halloumi on top of the tomatoes, sprinkle with the dried mint and drizzle with more olive oil.

Roast in the oven for about 20 minutes, until the tomatoes have softened and have started to break down, and the halloumi is lightly browned round the edges and softened inside.

Meanwhile, make the salad. Arrange the lettuce, cucumber, red onion and green pepper in a salad bowl or serving dish. Whisk the olive oil and vinegar together and season with salt and pepper. Pour this over the salad, then sprinkle over the olives, capers and oregano leaves. Squeeze over some lemon juice.

Add the tomatoes and halloumi with any juices from the dish – this will make a lovely warm dressing.

# Grilled vegetable & freekeh salad

**Freekeh**

150g cracked freekeh

1 tbsp olive oil

400ml vegetable stock or water

sea salt and black pepper

**Grilled vegetables**

2 courgettes, cut into thin strips on the diagonal

bunch of spring onions, trimmed

2 tbsp olive oil

**Dressing**

1 tbsp tahini

2 tbsp olive oil

juice and zest of 1 lemon

½ tsp maple syrup or pomegranate molasses

1 garlic clove, crushed

¼ tsp ground cinnamon

¼ tsp ground allspice

**Salad**

1 medium cucumber, finely diced

150g tomatoes, finely diced

large bunch of parsley, finely chopped

1 or more small bunches of mint, coriander or dill, finely chopped

20g pine nuts, lightly toasted

Freekeh may sound a bit, well, freaky but it's just a really nice grain, a bit like couscous and bulgur, and makes a good hearty base for a salad. We're recent converts and now it's a store cupboard essential for us both. We like to griddle the veg to get the charred look and taste, but if you prefer you can just pop them on a baking tray and cook them in the oven.

First cook the freekeh. Soak it for 5 minutes in plenty of cold water, then drain thoroughly. Heat the oil in a saucepan and add the freekeh. Toast until the freekeh is dry – it will give off steam to start with – then season with plenty of salt. Add 300ml of the stock or water and bring to the boil, then turn down the heat and cover. Simmer over a low heat for 15–20 minutes, until the freekeh is cooked and all the liquid has been absorbed. If it isn't quite done, add a splash more stock or water and continue cooking.

Next grill the vegetables. Heat a griddle pan until it's too hot to hold your hand over. Toss the courgettes and the spring onions in the oil and season with salt and pepper. Grill on each side until the vegetables have deep char lines and have softened. You may have to do this in more than one batch.

To make the dressing, whisk all the ingredients together with plenty of salt and pepper. Thin the dressing with a little water until it is about the consistency of single cream.

To assemble the salad, mix the freekeh with the cucumber, tomatoes and most of the herbs and pine nuts, reserving a few for a garnish. Toss with 2 tablespoons of the dressing. Roughly chop the grilled spring onions, or leave them whole if you like, and arrange them over the freekeh along with the courgettes. Top with more of the dressing and the reserved herbs and pine nuts, then serve.

SERVES 4

1 tbsp Thai sticky rice
(or jasmine or basmati)

75g fine green beans, very finely
sliced into 1mm rounds

2 tbsp groundnut oil

3 shallots, very finely sliced
into 1mm rounds

100g shiitake mushrooms,
very finely diced

50g tempeh, very finely diced

½ tsp dulse seaweed flakes
or ground seaweed

1 garlic clove, crushed

1 tsp chilli flakes

½ tsp light soft brown sugar

1 tbsp soy sauce

3 tbsp lime juice

leaves from a small bunch
of coriander

leaves from a small bunch of mint

leaves from 2 small little gem
lettuces

sea salt and black pepper

# Thai-spiced mushroom salad

**This is a vegan version of the Thai salad known as larb or laab and we really love it. It's usually made with minced chicken or pork, but this mushroom version is full of great flavour. The key to success is to chop everything as finely as you can. And don't be tempted to skip the ground rice – it adds great texture and flavour to the salad.**

First toast the rice. Put it into a dry frying pan and toast over a medium heat, shaking the pan regularly, until the rice is a warm golden brown and smelling nutty. Remove and cool down, then finely grind to a powder in a spice grinder or blender. Set aside.

Heat a small pan of water and add salt. Add the green beans and blanch them for 2–3 minutes until just al dente and still a bright green. Rinse them under a cold tap and drain thoroughly.

Heat half the oil in a large frying pan. Add the shallots and fry them over a medium heat until golden brown and crisp. Remove from the pan and set aside, then add the rest of the oil. Fry the mushrooms and tempeh with the seaweed, garlic and chilli flakes for several minutes until the mushrooms have reduced down and the mixture is dry. Add the sugar, soy sauce and lime juice.

Chop the herbs, keeping any tiny leaves whole. Put the shallots back in the pan along with the herbs. Taste and adjust the flavours as you like – you may want more lime juice, chilli, sugar or soy sauce. Add a few grinds of black pepper.

Serve the salad on little gem leaves with some of the rice powder sprinkled over the top.

2 bunches of asparagus, trimmed

1 tbsp olive oil

2 hard-boiled eggs, yolks and whites separated

1 tbsp capers, drained

sea salt and black pepper

**Dressing**

2 tbsp olive oil

1 tsp Dijon mustard

1 tbsp sherry vinegar

a few tarragon leaves, finely chopped

# Asparagus mimosa

Cooking asparagus on a griddle works brilliantly and provides great flavour, but you can steam your asparagus instead if you prefer. The yellow and white of the hard-boiled egg topping is said to resemble mimosa blossom – hence the name – and this elegant little salad is a delight to the eye and to the tum. Makes a wonderful starter for a posh dinner too.

Heat a griddle pan until it's too hot to hold your hand over for more than a few seconds. Toss the asparagus in the oil and season with plenty of salt and pepper. Place the asparagus on the hot griddle and grill for several minutes, turning regularly, until it is all tender and nicely charred.

Keeping the egg yolks and whites separate, chop them as finely as you can – you can also push them through a sieve if you want them extra fine. Whisk the dressing ingredients together and season with salt and pepper.

Arrange the asparagus on a serving dish or on separate plates, then drizzle over the dressing and add the capers. Sprinkle with the egg whites and top with the egg yolks. Serve the salad at room temperature.

600g tomatoes (use a mix of varieties and sizes if possible)

1 small red onion, very finely sliced

1 burrata or 2 fresh mozzarella balls

leaves from a small sprig of thyme

sea salt and black pepper

**Dressing**

small bunch of basil

2 tbsp olive oil

2 tsp sherry vinegar

# Tomato & burrata salad

Dave: this is our take on the classic tricolour salad and one of my favourites. It's the dish I make when my first homegrown tomatoes are ready. A totally luxurious and delicious soft Italian cheese, burrata is the real deal for this but obviously the salad is also great with mozzarella – check the one you buy is suitable for vegetarians. For the best flavour, keep your tomatoes out of the fridge. If they are cold, leave them to come to room temperature, preferably in the sun. Makes all the difference, as cold tomatoes are not nearly so tasty.

First prepare the tomatoes whichever way you like. Tiny cherry tomatoes can be left whole or halved, large tomatoes can be sliced or cut into wedges – it's up to you!

Arrange the tomatoes on a platter or in a shallow bowl, then add the red onion. Sprinkle over some salt and pepper and leave to stand while you make the dressing.

Pull off any very small leaves from the basil and reserve them for the salad. Put the large leaves, discarding the stems, into a small food processor with the olive oil and sherry vinegar. Season with salt and pepper, then process. Check every few seconds – you want a green-flecked sauce rather than one that is completely smooth.

Pour most of the dressing over the tomatoes and gently fold together. Add the burrata to the salad and gently break it open at the top (if using mozzarella, just pull the balls into pieces). Garnish with the thyme and the reserved basil, then drizzle over the remaining dressing. Serve immediately with some good bread.

# American-style layered salad

250g new/salad potatoes, scraped or skin on

4 spring onions

small sprig of tarragon, finely chopped

1 small romaine lettuce or half an iceberg, shredded

1 medium carrot, coarsely grated

¼ red cabbage, shredded

bunch of radishes, diced

200g tomatoes, diced

## Dressing

100ml buttermilk

50g crème fraiche or yoghurt

1 tbsp olive oil

1 tsp Dijon mustard

1 tbsp cider vinegar

½ tsp garlic powder

1 small garlic clove, crushed or grated

sea salt and black pepper

## Toppings

100g vegetarian Cheddar or similar, grated

2 hard-boiled eggs, yolks and whites separated

50g tofu bacon bits (see p.266)

a few chives, finely snipped

**This is a proper hearty salad that makes a great meal on a summer day – or any day. You can serve it American-style layered up in a glass bowl, or you can arrange the different elements in rows on a big platter, then sprinkle over the toppings – the 'bacon' bits are genius. However you serve it, you'll love eating this salad.**

First cook the potatoes in plenty of boiling water until tender, then drain. While the potatoes are cooking, make the dressing by whisking everything together and seasoning with salt and pepper. If the dressing is on the thick side – it should have a pourable consistency similar to that of double cream – thin it with a little water. Spoon a tablespoon of the dressing over the warm potatoes and toss with the spring onions and tarragon.

To assemble the salad, arrange the lettuce, carrot, cabbage, radishes, tomatoes and potato salad in rows or layers and sprinkle with the cheese. If layering the salad, put the potato salad on top before sprinkling over the cheese.

Finely chop the egg whites and yolks separately as finely as you can, then sprinkle the whites over the salad. Drizzle over most of the dressing, then top with the egg yolks, tofu bacon bits and the chives. Serve with any remaining dressing on the side.

Soups

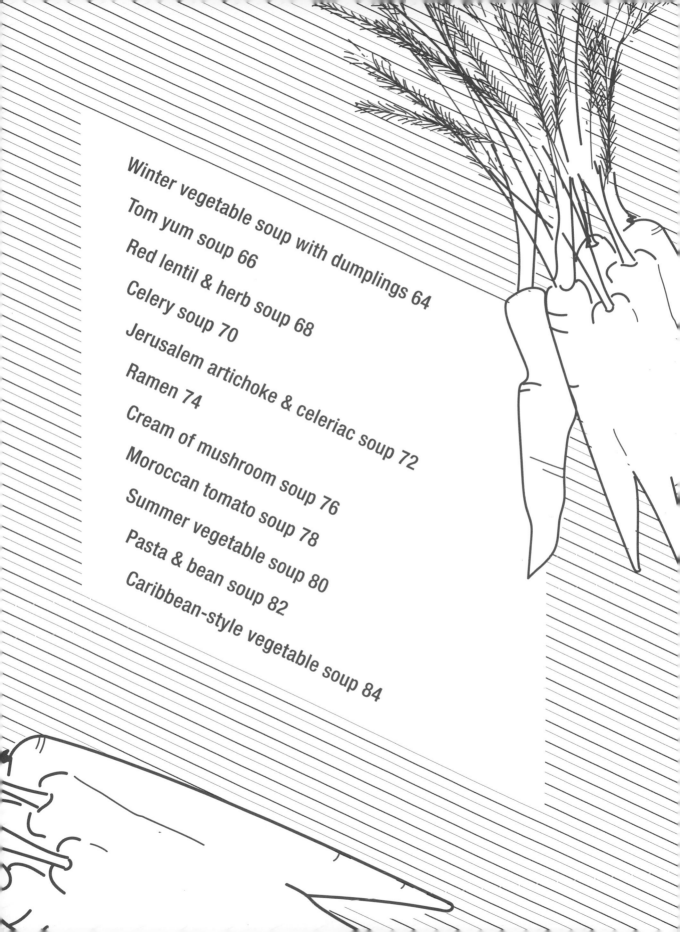

Winter vegetable soup with dumplings 64

Tom yum soup 66

Red lentil & herb soup 68

Celery soup 70

Jerusalem artichoke & celeriac soup 72

Ramen 74

Cream of mushroom soup 76

Moroccan tomato soup 78

Summer vegetable soup 80

Pasta & bean soup 82

Caribbean-style vegetable soup 84

# Winter vegetable soup with dumplings

2 tbsp olive oil

1 onion, finely chopped

1 celery stick, finely chopped

600g root vegetables, such as carrots, parsnips, swede, turnips, celeriac and potatoes, sliced or diced

150g beetroots (100g peeled and diced, 50g grated)

3 garlic cloves, finely chopped

1 tsp dried thyme or 2 sprigs of fresh

50g barley

up to 1.5 litres vegetable stock

1 tsp Marmite

2 leeks, finely sliced

100g kale, shredded

sea salt and black pepper

**Dumplings**

150g self-raising flour

75g butter or vegetarian suet

1 tsp caraway seeds (optional)

1 tsp dried thyme

**To serve**

finely chopped dill or parsley

mustard or horseradish

We both love a dumpling and this is a really hearty soup for a winter's day – a proper Hairy Biker dinner. You can use butter for the dumplings, which makes them lovely and light, but if you want this to be a vegan dish use vegetarian suet. And if you don't fancy caraway seeds, try adding some chopped dill to the mix. Use whatever root veg you like, but go easy on the potato.

Heat the oil in a saucepan or a flameproof casserole dish. Add the onion and cook gently over a medium-high heat until it starts to take on some colour. Add the rest of the veg, including the diced beetroot, but not the grated, and continue to cook, stirring regularly, for another 10 minutes until they start to reduce in volume.

Stir in the garlic, thyme and barley and cook for another couple of minutes. Pour in 1.2 litres of the stock and season. Bring to the boil, then turn down to a fast simmer. Stir in the Marmite (the heat will melt it off the spoon) and partially cover the pan with a lid. Simmer for about 20 minutes until the vegetables start to soften.

Add the leeks and kale. Continue to cook until the barley is swollen and slightly al dente and the vegetables are tender – this should take 15–20 minutes. Add more liquid if the soup gets too thick.

Meanwhile, make the dumplings. If you want the dumplings firm and lightly browned, preheat the oven to 200°C/Fan 180°C/Gas 6, or you can just steam them on top of the soup.

Put the flour into a bowl and add the butter or suet. Rub in the fat, then season well. Add the caraway seeds, if using, and the thyme and just enough water to make a slightly tacky dough. Divide the dough into 8 pieces and roll it into balls.

Stir the grated beetroot into the soup. Drop the dumplings on top of the soup and either put the pan in the oven for about 15 minutes until the dumplings are puffed up and lightly browned, or cover and leave to simmer on the hob for 15–20 minutes. Garnish with dill or parsley and serve with dollops of mustard or horseradish.

# Tom yum soup

Lots of ingredients we know, but you'll find them all in the supermarket and this is easy to cook and well worth it – make double the broth and stash some away in the freezer. You're going to love the flavours of our vegan version of a Thai hot and sour soup. Thai basil is best here, but if you can't find any, use the ordinary sort. And the amount of fresh chilli you use depends on how hot they are and your taste buds.

**Paste**

2 shallots, peeled

2 hot dried chillies

2–4 fresh red chillies

4 garlic cloves, roughly chopped

25g galangal or fresh root ginger, roughly chopped

2 lemongrass stalks, roughly chopped

zest of 1 lime

6 lime leaves

**Broth**

1 carrot

4 heads of pak choi or similar

12 cherry tomatoes

4 lime leaves

1 bunch of coriander, stems and leaves separated

4 spring onions, to garnish

1 tbsp coconut oil

1 onion, finely sliced

1 litre vegetable stock

1 lemongrass stalk, left whole and bruised

200ml coconut milk

2 tbsp soy sauce

juice of 1 lime

1 tsp light soft brown sugar

1 block of silken tofu, carefully cut into cubes and brought up to room temperature

small bunch of Thai or regular basil

sea salt and black pepper

**To serve**

lime wedges

chilli oil

First make the paste. Put the shallots, dried chillies and fresh chillies into a frying pan and dry fry them for several minutes until they have started to blacken and smell very aromatic. Remove from the heat and set aside to cool.

Put them in a food processor with all the remaining paste ingredients and blitz to make a bright red paste. Keep pulsing and scraping down the sides of the bowl regularly. If you're having trouble, add a couple of tablespoons of water.

For the broth, slice the carrot into ribbons with a potato peeler and cut the pak choi into thin pieces lengthways. Cut the tomatoes in half. Shred the lime leaves very finely – no larger than $^{1}/_{2}$mm – and finely chop the coriander stems. Cut the spring onions in half lengthways, then shred into pieces no larger than 1mm.

Heat the coconut oil in a large saucepan. Add the onion, fry for a few minutes over a medium heat until it is a light golden brown, then add the paste. Fry for a few minutes, then add the stock and lemongrass. Bring to the boil and simmer for 5 minutes.

Add the coconut milk, soy sauce, lime juice and sugar. Stir to combine and to dissolve the sugar, then add the carrot ribbons, pak choi, cherry tomatoes, lime leaves and coriander stems. Check for seasoning and add salt and pepper as necessary, then simmer until the vegetables are tender. Taste again and add more seasoning, lime juice and sugar to taste.

Divide the tofu between 4 large bowls. Ladle over the broth, then garnish with the spring onions, coriander leaves and basil leaves. Serve with lime wedges and chilli oil to make it extra hot.

# Red lentil & herb soup

3 tbsp olive oil
1 large onion, finely chopped
3 fat garlic cloves, finely chopped
small bunch of parsley
small bunch of coriander
small bunch of dill (optional)
1 tsp dried mint
200g red lentils, well rinsed
1 litre vegetable stock or water
zest and juice of ½ lemon
sea salt and black pepper

This is a nice straightforward soup, which is good and hearty because of the lentils but also full of the fresh taste of herbs. A real keeper. If you like, you could add some fresh spinach at the last minute and just let it wilt into the soup. Frozen spinach works fine too.

Heat the oil in a large pan and add the onion. Cook over a gentle heat until completely soft and translucent, then turn up the heat for a few minutes to allow the onion to caramelise around the edges. Add the garlic and cook for a further 2 minutes.

Pick off any large stems from the herbs and tie them together. Add the bunch of stems to the pan along with the dried mint, lentils and stock. Season with plenty of salt and pepper. Bring the soup to the boil, then turn down the heat to a fairly fast simmer and partially cover the pan. Leave to cook until the lentils have broken down into a thin purée. Remove the herb stems and check the consistency. If the soup is a little too thick for your liking, add more stock or water.

Finely chop the remaining herbs and stir them into the soup with the lemon zest and juice. Simmer for another couple of minutes, then taste for seasoning. Add more salt, pepper or lemon juice to taste, then serve.

2 tbsp olive oil

1 small onion, finely chopped

400g celery, finely sliced

1 small or medium floury potato (about 150g), finely diced

½ tsp celery or sea salt (or to taste)

2 garlic cloves, finely chopped

600ml vegetable stock

100ml whole milk

**Garnish**

olive oil, for frying

celery leaves

celery salt

# Celery soup

Celery soup is a real classic and not one you see so often these days. We both love it. If possible, it's good to buy a proper head of leafy celery for this, rather than the packs of hearts or celery sticks. If the celery is nice and fresh the leaves will be beautifully green and fry well. We recommend canning the can and making this.

---

Heat the oil in a saucepan and add the onion, celery and potato. Sprinkle with celery salt or ordinary sea salt and stir well to coat everything with the oil. Cover the pan with a lid and cook over a low to medium heat, stirring at regular intervals, until the veg are glossy and transparent. This will take 10–15 minutes.

Add the garlic and stir for a couple of minutes, then pour in the stock. Bring to the boil, then turn the heat down to a simmer and cover the pan. Simmer for another 5–10 minutes until the vegetables are completely tender.

Pour in the milk and remove the pan from the heat. Blitz with a hand-held blender or in a jug blender. If you want a completely smooth soup, pass it through a sieve. Reheat gently, taste for seasoning and adjust as necessary.

For the garnish, coat the base of a small frying pan or saucepan with ½cm of olive oil. Heat the oil, then add the celery leaves and fry until crisp and glossy. Remove with a slotted spoon and drain on kitchen paper, then sprinkle with celery salt.

Serve the soup garnished with the crisp celery leaves.

 **BIKER VEGAN TIP**

No need for cream in this recipe, which means it works brilliantly as a vegan dish if you use unsweetened plant-based milk instead of regular milk.

# Jerusalem artichoke & celeriac soup

2 tbsp olive oil

1 onion, finely chopped

250g Jerusalem artichokes, diced

150g floury potatoes, diced

150g celeriac, diced

3 garlic cloves, finely chopped

1 large sprig of thyme, left whole

leaves from 2 sprigs of rosemary,
  very finely chopped

1 litre vegetable stock

sea salt and black pepper

**Rosemary oil garnish (optional)**

2 tbsp olive oil

leaves from a rosemary sprig

squeeze of lemon juice

These two knobbly winter veg wouldn't win a beauty contest but they sure score on flavour and make good bedfellows in a soup. We like to leave this a bit chunky rather than blitzed to super smooth, but your choice. The rosemary oil garnish is a doddle to make and adds a classy finishing touch.

Heat the oil in a large saucepan and add the onion, Jerusalem artichokes, potatoes and celeriac. Cook gently over a medium to high heat, stirring regularly, for up to 10 minutes, until everything has taken on some colour around the edges. Add the garlic and cook for another 2 minutes.

Add the herbs and stock and season generously with salt and pepper. Bring to the boil, then turn down the heat and partially cover the pan. Simmer until the vegetables are very tender and break up easily when squashed on the side of the pan.

Break up some of the diced vegetables with a masher – this will thicken the soup a little without having to purée it and keeps some nice texture. If you do want a smooth soup, blitz it with a blender.

For the garnish, heat the oil in a pan and add the rosemary. It will quickly brown and crisp up, then remove it and add a squeeze of lemon and a pinch of salt. Drizzle some of the flavoured oil over each portion of soup.

## Broth

1 x 10g piece of kombu,
   soaked for half an hour in cold
   water OR 2 tsp seaweed flakes

15g dried shiitake mushrooms

4 garlic cloves, thinly sliced

25g fresh root ginger, thinly sliced

1 tbsp caster sugar

50ml soy sauce

3 tbsp mirin or sake

1 tbsp miso paste

## Soup

1 tbsp vegetable oil

1 Chinese cabbage,
   cut into slim wedges

1 onion, coarsely sliced from
   top to bottom

1 large carrot, cut into ½cm
   slices on the diagonal

1 tsp miso paste

6 spring onions, whites cut on the
   diagonal, greens very finely sliced

## To serve

4 nests of noodles

a few drops of sesame oil

4 sheets of nori sushi seaweed,
   roughly torn

4 tamago eggs, halved
   (optional – see p.265)

sesame seeds

## To garnish

a few sprigs of coriander

4 handfuls of bean sprouts (optional)

chilli oil

soy sauce

# Ramen

This recipe shows that you can make a good ramen with veggie broth. There are two options for our version of the classic Japanese noodle soup. You can add delicious tamago eggs (see page 265) at the end or make it vegan by using crisp fried tofu instead – see our tip. Both are great, so take your pick. If you opt for the eggs, they do need to be made in advance.

---

Put all the broth ingredients into a saucepan and add 1.5 litres of water. Bring to the boil, then turn the heat down and simmer for 30 minutes until everything is very soft and the stock has reduced by about a third. Remove from the heat and leave to stand.

In a separate pan, start the soup by heating the oil. Add the cabbage and fry it over a high heat until lightly browned on the cut sides, then remove from the pan and set aside. Add the onion and carrot and cook until the onion is lightly browned. Stir in the miso paste to coat the vegetables and cook for a further couple of minutes. Put the cabbage back into the pan.

Strain the broth and pour it over the vegetables. Check the seasoning and add more soy, mirin or sugar to taste. Add the white parts of the spring onions and simmer until the cabbage is tender.

Cook the noodles according to the packet instructions, then run them under a cold tap and drain thoroughly. Toss them in the sesame oil. Divide the noodles and nori sheets between 4 large bowls, then ladle over the broth and vegetables. Sprinkle the sesame seeds over the eggs, if using, and add these to the bowls, then garnish with the spring onion greens, coriander and bean sprouts, if using. Serve with chilli oil and more soy sauce.

 **BIKER VEGAN TIP**

For a vegan ramen, cut a block of extra-firm tofu into chunks, pat them dry and toss in a tablespoon of cornflour. Heat a tablespoon of vegetable oil in a frying pan and fry the tofu until crisp and browned on all sides. Drizzle with a few drops of sesame oil and sprinkle with sesame seeds. Add the fried tofu to the soup instead of the eggs.

SERVES 4

1 tbsp olive oil

25g butter

1 onion, finely chopped

1 leek, whites only, finely sliced

500g mushrooms (mixture of field, white, portobello and chestnut), finely chopped

3 garlic cloves, finely chopped

leaves from a few sprigs of tarragon, roughly chopped

900ml water or vegetable or mushroom stock

1 tbsp sherry (oloroso or similar) or marsala, to taste

sea salt and black pepper

**To garnish**

finely chopped tarragon

100ml single cream

# Cream of mushroom soup

Another classic this one and very easy to make. It's good to use a mixture of mushrooms as we've suggested, and they don't need to be anything fancy – although a few shiitake are a good addition if you have some. It's well worth using a nice glug of sherry or marsala too, if poss, and it adds a nice depth of flavour. Serve this up, add a beautiful swirl of cream and you'll have a fancy-looking dish.

Heat the oil and butter in a large saucepan. When the butter starts to foam, add the onion and leek and cook over a gentle heat until both are soft and translucent. Turn up the heat to medium-high and add the mushrooms. Season with salt and pepper.

Cook until the mushrooms have reduced down in volume by about a third, then add the garlic and tarragon. Continue to stir for a minute or so, then pour in the water or stock. Bring the soup to the boil, then turn the heat down and simmer for 10 minutes or until everything is tender. Add the sherry and simmer for another minute.

Remove the pan from the heat. Purée in a blender or with a stick blender until the soup is flecked and still very slightly textured. Remove 2 or 3 ladlefuls of the soup and continue to blend the rest until it is completely smooth. Pour all the soup back into the pan. Check for seasoning and add more salt and pepper as necessary.

For the garnish, add the tarragon and a pinch of salt to the cream and whisk very lightly until frothy and aerated but still liquid – this will help the cream float on top of the soup instead of sinking in. Drizzle the cream in a swirl on each serving of soup and top with a few more snips of tarragon.

2 tbsp olive oil

1 large onion, finely chopped

200g butternut squash,
    peeled and finely diced

2 large garlic cloves,
    finely chopped or crushed

2 tbsp red harissa paste

50g red lentils, well rinsed

400g can of tomatoes

800ml vegetable stock or water

sea salt and black pepper

**Garnish**

1 tbsp olive oil

150g cooked chickpeas
    (canned or see p.270)

1 tsp harissa paste

1 tbsp lemon juice

small bunch of parsley,
    finely chopped

# Moroccan tomato soup

Good old tomato is a favourite soup and we've made lots of different versions. We're really happy with this recipe, which has a nice touch of North African flavour. Harissa paste is made of chilli and lots of spices and herbs and adds a great punch to any dish. It's available in supermarkets.

Heat the oil in a large saucepan. Add the onion and cook over a low to medium heat until translucent. Add the squash and garlic and cook for several more minutes.

Stir in the harissa paste and the lentils. Mix thoroughly, then add the tomatoes and stock. Season with plenty of salt and pepper.

Bring to the boil, then reduce the heat to a steady simmer and partially cover the pan. Leave to simmer until the lentils and butternut squash are tender – about 20 minutes. Purée the soup with a stick blender or in a jug blender, then taste for seasoning.

To make the garnish, heat the oil in a frying pan and add the chickpeas. Season with plenty of salt and pepper and stir in the harissa paste. Add the lemon juice, then cook, stirring constantly, until the pan looks dry.

Serve the soup garnished with the fried chickpeas and some chopped parsley.

SERVES 4

# Summer vegetable soup

This really is a celebration of summer, using all those lovely veg, such as courgettes, lettuce, peas and asparagus when they are at their best. It's topped with some pea and mint pesto to add extra colour and texture and it's a delight to eat. If you have an allotment, this is a great way of making the most of your homegrown beauties. You can, of course, use frozen peas and beans if you prefer, and the soup will still be delicious.

1 tbsp olive oil

15g butter

2 leeks, sliced

400g new/salad potatoes,
    cut into ½ cm slices

50ml vermouth

750ml vegetable stock

bouquet garni (2 tarragon sprigs,
    2 oregano sprigs, 2 strips of
    pared lemon zest tied together)

2 small courgettes, sliced into rounds

1 fat or 2 regular little gem lettuces,
    cut into 8–12 wedges

12 asparagus spears, trimmed

50g peas

50g baby broad beans
    (no need to peel)

squeeze of lemon juice

a few small basil leaves, to garnish

sea salt and black pepper

**Pea and mint pesto**

75g peas

20g vegetarian hard cheese, grated

½ tsp dried mint

1 tbsp olive oil

1 tsp tarragon mustard

squeeze of lemon juice

Heat the oil and butter in a large saucepan. When the butter has melted, add the leeks and potatoes. Stir until everything is glossy and coated with butter, then cook gently for 5 minutes. Season with salt and pepper. Add the vermouth, bring to the boil, then turn down the heat and cover the pan. Leave to braise for another 5 minutes or until the leeks and potatoes are perfectly tender.

Add the stock and bouquet garni to the pan, together with the courgettes and little gems. Bring to the boil again, then turn down the heat and simmer for 5 minutes. Add the asparagus, peas and broad beans and simmer until the asparagus is just cooked. It should be al dente and still a fresh green colour after 2 or 3 minutes. Taste for seasoning and add more salt, pepper and a squeeze of lemon juice.

To make the pesto, blitz everything in a food processor to make a rough purée. Season with plenty of salt and pepper.

Remove the bouquet garni and serve the soup with spoonfuls of the pesto dropped into it and garnish with a few basil leaves.

 **BIKER VEGAN TIP**

It's easy to make this a vegan soup. Just use extra oil instead of the butter, and make the pesto with 20g of toasted pine nuts instead of cheese.

3 tbsp olive oil

1 large onion, finely chopped

2 celery sticks, finely chopped

4 garlic cloves, finely chopped

needles from several sprigs
   of rosemary, finely chopped

3 bay leaves

small bunch of parsley, leaves and
   stems separated, finely chopped

½ tsp chilli flakes

500g cooked beans (borlotti or
   cannellini) or 2 x 400g cans,
   drained

120g short pasta tubes,
   such as casarecce or ditali

small bunch of greens, shredded
   (chard, kale, spring greens,
   something wintery)

1 courgette, finely sliced

sea salt and black pepper

**To serve (optional)**

squeeze of lemon

extra chilli flakes

vegetarian hard cheese,
   grated or shaved

# Pasta & bean soup

This is our version of a much-loved Italian classic called pasta e fagioli. It's pretty much a store-cupboard dish – you don't have to add fresh greens but they are nice – and there is nothing more comforting or warming on a cool night. The hit of chilli is so good and you can also add a touch of lemon juice if you like – not traditional but we like it.

---

Heat the oil in a large saucepan. Add the onion and celery, put a lid on the pan and cook very gently until soft and translucent. Add half the garlic and rosemary, then the bay leaves, parsley stems and chilli flakes, and cook for another couple of minutes.

Measure a litre of water. Use a ladleful of it to moisten a third of the beans, then purée them roughly so they are broken up but not smooth. Add these and the whole beans to the pan with the rest of the water. Season generously and bring to the boil. Simmer for 5 minutes.

Add the pasta, shredded greens and courgette to the pan. Bring back to the boil, then turn the heat down to a simmer. After about 5 minutes, add the remaining garlic and rosemary, then continue to cook until the pasta is al dente and the courgettes are well on their way to breaking down.

Sprinkle with the parsley leaves and serve with a little squeeze of lemon, extra chilli flakes and plenty of cheese, if using.

 **BIKER VEGAN TIP**

Simply leave out the cheese and this is a great vegan meal.

# Caribbean-style vegetable soup

1 tbsp coconut oil

1 onion, diced

1 large carrot, diced

1 red pepper, deseeded and diced

1 green pepper, deseeded and diced

1 small aubergine, diced

150g pumpkin or sweet potato, diced

¼ white or green cabbage,
    finely shredded

2 tsp Caribbean curry powder
    (or medium/mild curry powder)

3 garlic cloves, finely chopped

1 tsp ground allspice

2 bay leaves

large sprig of thyme

1 scotch bonnet, left whole

400ml coconut milk

600ml vegetable stock or water

1 tbsp soy sauce

25g basmati rice, rinsed

400g can of red kidney beans,
    drained

sea salt and black pepper

**To garnish**

lime wedges, for squeezing

There's a definite sunshine vibe to this soup, with its Caribbean flavours of spices, scotch bonnet and coconut milk. It's easy to make but for best results, just make sure you cut the veg into small dice – about a centimetre square should do nicely. Once that's done the rest is simple. This is a wonderful example of the great gifts to cooking from our multicultural society.

Heat the oil in a large saucepan. Add all the vegetables and cook over a medium heat for about 10 minutes until the volume has started to reduce and they are softening around the edges.

Stir in the curry powder, garlic, allspice, bay and thyme and stir for a minute or so until the vegetables are well coated with the spices. Add the scotch bonnet and season generously with salt and pepper. Pour in the coconut milk, stock or water and the soy sauce and sprinkle in the rice and the kidney beans.

Bring to the boil, then turn down the heat to a simmer and cover the pan. Simmer for 20–25 minutes until the vegetables are tender and starting to collapse and the rice is cooked through. Taste for seasoning and adjust accordingly.

Fish out the scotch bonnet, bay leaves and thyme sprigs and serve with a generous squeeze of lime juice.

Snacks & light dishes

Tomato fritters 90

Cheese & Marmite scones 92

Cheese & tomato savoury cakes 94

Biker blinis 96

Vegan sausage rolls 98

Potstickers 100

Artichoke & basil dip 102

Red pepper hummus 102

Tempeh shawarma 104

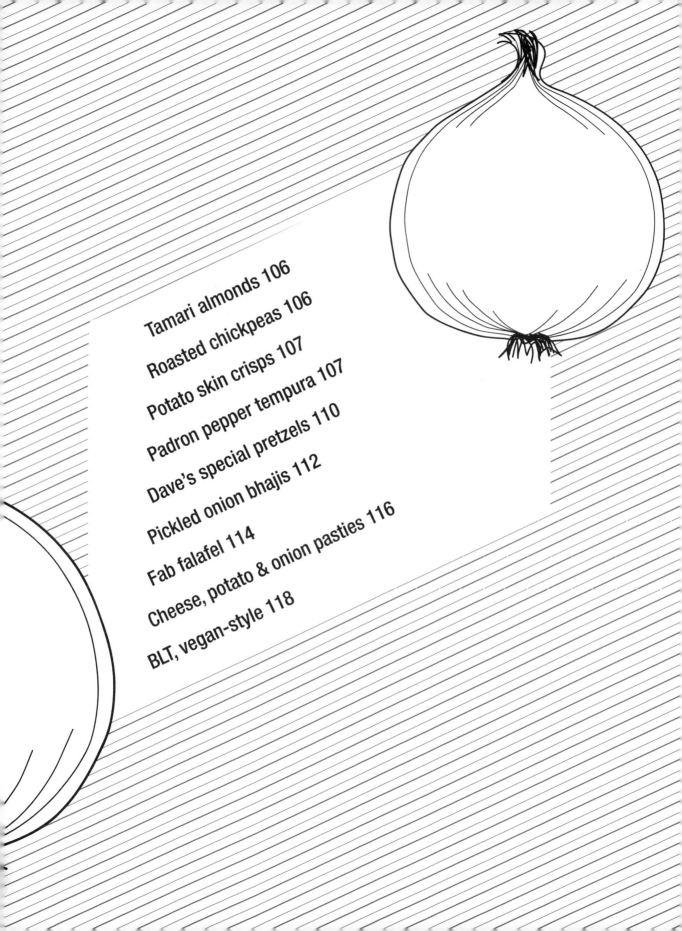

Tamari almonds 106

Roasted chickpeas 106

Potato skin crisps 107

Padron pepper tempura 107

Dave's special pretzels 110

Pickled onion bhajis 112

Fab falafel 114

Cheese, potato & onion pasties 116

BLT, vegan-style 118

SERVES 4

400g cherry tomatoes, cut into 8 pieces

1 small red onion, very finely diced

150g plain flour

2 tsp baking powder

1 tsp ground cinnamon

1 tsp dried oregano

1 tsp dried mint

1 tsp tomato ketchup

1 tsp mushroom ketchup

small bunch of dill, fronds roughly chopped

1 egg

vegetable oil, for deep-frying

sea salt and black pepper

**To serve**

250ml Greek yoghurt

small bunch of dill, finely chopped

1 tsp white wine vinegar

pinch of sugar

# Tomato fritters

**Fritters make a brilliant little snack and these are flipping delicious. Great with the dill and yoghurt dip.**

Put the diced tomatoes in a sieve with the red onion and sprinkle over half a teaspoon of salt. Set the sieve over a bowl to collect any liquid and leave to stand for half an hour.

Put the flour in a bowl with the baking powder, cinnamon and dried herbs. Season with plenty of salt and pepper. Add the tomatoes and onion, along with the ketchups, dill and the egg. Measure the strained tomato liquid and make it up to 50ml with water. Add it a tablespoon at a time to the batter until it is still quite thick but loose enough to drop slowly from a spoon. You may not need all the liquid.

Add oil to a deep-fat fryer or a large saucepan. If using a saucepan, make sure you don't fill it above halfway – the oil should be about 5cm deep. Heat the oil to 180°C. Drop heaped dessertspoons of the batter into the oil, a few at a time. They will fry quickly so give them just a minute or two on each side. When the fritters are slightly puffed up, crisp, and a light golden brown, remove with a slotted spoon and drain on kitchen paper.

Mix the yoghurt with the dill, white wine vinegar and sugar. Season with salt and pepper and serve with the tomato fritters.

 **BIKER VEGAN TIP**

To make this recipe vegan, use 50m of aquafaba (the liquid from a can of unsalted chickpeas) instead of the egg. This works perfectly well, but the fritters will be slightly more fragile, so take extra care when frying. Use plant-based yoghurt for the dip.

150ml whole milk

1 tbsp Marmite

300g self-raising flour,
    plus extra for dusting

1 tsp baking powder

½ tsp salt

85g butter, chilled and cubed

150g vegetarian hard cheese
    (such as Cheddar), coarsely grated

1 tsp mustard powder

1 tbsp caster sugar

# Cheese & Marmite scones

**We do like a scone, and these cheese and Marmite ones are the business – proper craggy and tasty but also light as a feather. Take care, though, not to mix the dough too much or your scones will be more use as hand grenades than for tea with the vicar. Top tip is to not to twist the cutter as you press it down into the dough. This helps prevent the scones from turning out lopsided – but to be honest, they still taste great, lopsided or not. Carnivore or vegetarian you have to love these.**

First heat the milk in a pan until it is just starting to feel hot – blood temperature (a bit hotter than tepid). Whisk in the Marmite until it has combined completely with the milk – the milk should turn a colour similar to milky coffee. Remove the pan from the heat and leave to cool down. If you have time, chill it as well, but don't worry too much if you can't.

Mix the flour, baking powder and salt in a bowl. Add the butter and rub it in until the mixture is the texture of fine breadcrumbs. Add the grated cheese, mustard powder and sugar, then, if time allows, leave the mixture in the fridge to chill for half an hour.

Preheat the oven to 220°C/Fan 200°C/Gas 7. Line a baking tray with baking paper.

Reserve a tablespoon of the milk and Marmite mixture for a glaze and pour the rest into the bowl of dry ingredients. Mix everything together as quickly as you can, using either a table knife or your fingers. Don't overwork the dough or the scones will be tough.

Turn the dough out on to a floured work surface and pat it down until it is about 3cm thick – do this with your hands, no need for a rolling pin. Dip a 6cm cutter in flour and cut out rounds, pushing the cutter straight down. Squash the remaining dough together and cut out more scones. You should end up with 8 or 9.

Put the scones on the baking tray and brush with the reserved milk and Marmite. Bake for 12–15 minutes until they are well risen and deep golden brown. Eat hot or cold, with lots of butter.

# Cheese & tomato savoury cakes

200g plain flour

1½ tsp baking powder

1 tsp mustard powder

1 tsp dried oregano

150g vegetarian hard cheese
(such as Cheddar), grated

60ml olive oil

100ml Greek yoghurt

3 eggs

sea salt and black pepper

**Topping**

200g cherry tomatoes, halved or
left whole, depending on size

a few basil leaves

1 tbsp pumpkin seeds

25g vegetarian hard cheese
(such as Cheddar), grated

So simple and yet so tasty, savoury cakes are popular in France, where Dave first ate them and became a fan, and you see them with lots of different flavours. Our muffin-like versions make a cracking little snack on their own or slathered with some butter, cream cheese or Marmite. Be careful not to work the mixture too much or the result will be tough. The less you mix, the more tender the crumb. These are lovely French-style with aperitifs and also great for popping in your lunchbox.

---

Preheat the oven to 200°C/Fan 180°C/Gas 6. Line a 12-hole muffin pan with paper cases.

Mix the flour, baking powder, mustard powder, oregano and cheese together in a large bowl and stir in half a teaspoon of salt and a few twists of black pepper. In a separate bowl, whisk together the oil, yoghurt and eggs. Stir the wet ingredients into the dry ingredients, keeping mixing to a minimum.

Put a heaped tablespoon of the mixture into each paper case. Add 5 or 6 pieces of cherry tomato to each one, pushing some right down under the batter and pressing others into the top. Don't sit them on top without pressing them in as they won't sink. Place basil leaves under some of the pieces of tomato on top, then sprinkle with pumpkin seeds and more grated cheese.

Bake in the oven for 20–25 minutes until the cakes have risen and are lightly browned and the tomatoes are soft. Good served hot or cold on their own, or spread with butter or cream cheese.

100g buckwheat flour
50g strong white flour
½ tsp instant dried yeast
½ tsp salt
150ml whole milk
100ml soured cream or
    Greek yoghurt
2 eggs, separated
butter, for frying

**To serve**
200g vegetarian cream cheese
a handful of basil and mint leaves
½ jar of tapenade
16 cherry tomatoes, finely chopped
olive oil
sea salt and black pepper

# Biker blinis

**The secret to a good blini is to use buckwheat flour with its distinctive, slightly sour flavour. These are blinis you can really get your teeth into – not those dinky little cocktail jobs. Topped with some nicely seasoned cream cheese and olive tapenade, these are blini marvellous.**

Put both flours into a bowl. Add the yeast and mix, then add the salt and mix again.

Pour the milk into a pan and heat gently until blood temperature (a bit hotter than tepid). Remove from the heat and whisk in the soured cream or yoghurt and the egg yolks. Add the wet ingredients to the dry and stir well. Cover the bowl with a cloth or cling film and leave it somewhere warm until the mixture looks very well aerated. This will take up to 2 hours.

Whisk the egg whites to stiff peaks. Add a large tablespoon of the egg whites to the batter and stir, then fold in the rest, trying to keep as much volume as possible. Cover and leave for another hour – the mixture will aerate again.

Heat a small knob of butter in a large frying pan. Add large tablespoons of the batter to the pan and swirl into thin rounds, making sure they are well spaced out. Don't worry if they aren't perfectly round – it's all part of the charm. Flip the blinis over when the air bubbles have burst all over the surface, then cook on the other side. They should take about a minute per side. Continue frying the blinis, adding a little more butter each time. Allow to cool to room temperature.

To assemble, mix the cream cheese with some salt and pepper. Set aside a few tiny basil and mint leaves for a garnish, then finely chop the rest and mix with the cream cheese.

Spread a teaspoon of the cream cheese over each blini, then top with a swirl of tapenade and some chopped tomatoes. Drizzle over a little oil and top with the reserved basil and mint leaves.

MAKES 24

## Sausage mixture

5 tbsp olive oil

2–3 onions (about 200g),
    very finely chopped

1 large aubergine (about 250g),
    finely diced

200g cooked brown lentils,
    roughly puréed

100g walnuts, finely ground

100g very fine, dry breadcrumbs

75g oatmeal

2 tsp dried sage

½ tsp dried oregano

½ tsp dried thyme

½ tsp celery seeds

a few rasps of nutmeg

2 tbsp maple syrup

1 tbsp mushroom ketchup

sea salt and black pepper

## Rolls

2 sheets of vegan puff pastry

HP sauce or Dijon mustard,
    for spreading (optional)

1 tbsp vegetable oil

1 tbsp plant-based milk

# Vegan sausage rolls

Lots of people, including us, love the vegan sausage rolls from a certain high street bakery, but we wanted to have a shot at making our own. We've worked hard at this one and we're really chuffed with the flavour and texture. You can also make the mixture into sausages to cook on their own, add to the farmhouse hash (see page 26), or serve glazed with BBQ sauce (see page 200). Whatever you choose, you'll love these.

Heat 2 tablespoons of the oil in a frying pan. Add the onions and fry them over a low to medium heat until they are very soft and translucent. Turn up the heat and continue to cook until they are well caramelised – they should be a fairly uniform golden brown. Set aside.

Heat the remaining oil in a frying pan. Add the aubergine and fry over a medium to high heat initially, stirring frequently, until the aubergines are well browned round the edges. Then lower the heat and continue to cook until the pieces of aubergine are tender and have considerably reduced in volume.

Put the onions and aubergines in a food processor and pulse briefly to break them down a bit – you don't want a smooth purée. Tip the mixture into a bowl, then add the rest of the ingredients and season well. Mix well – it will seem dry at first but keep at it.

To make the sausage rolls, preheat the oven to 200°C/Fan 180°C/Gas 6. Line a baking tray with baking paper. Divide the sausage mixture into 4 pieces and shape each piece into rolls the length of the short side of the puff pastry – about 24cm.

Unroll a sheet of puff pastry. Spread with the HP sauce or mustard, if using, and arrange one of the rolls of sausage mixture along the short side, leaving a 4cm border all round. Roll the pastry over the sausage until the mixture is completely covered and there's at least another 1cm of pastry overlapping. Cut off the remaining pastry and press the join firmly together to seal. Repeat with a second roll of sausage mixture, setting aside any trimmings of pastry.

Repeat with the second sheet of pastry and the remaining 2 rolls of sausage mixture. Cut each roll into 6 pieces to give you 24 sausage rolls in total. Arrange the sausage rolls on the prepared baking tray. Mix the oil and milk together and brush over the rolls to glaze.

Bake for about 25 minutes until the sausage rolls are golden brown. Enjoy hot or cold.

To make sausages, divide the mixture into either 8 fat sausages (about 10cm long by 3cm in diameter), or 16 slim chipolatas (about 12cm long by 2cm in diameter). Wet your hands first, as this will make them easier to shape. Make sure you do this as soon as possible after making the mixture, as it will become dry quickly.

Wrap each sausage tightly in lightly oiled foil, making sure it is well sealed, and put the sausages in a steamer basket. Steam the fat sausages for 40 minutes, the slim ones for 25 minutes. Remove from the steamer basket and leave to cool completely – don't worry if they feel soft, they will firm up as they cool. Once cool, fry in a little oil until crisp.

pack of gyoza wrappers or
   make your own (see p.267)

**Filling**

1 tbsp olive oil

100g Chinese cabbage, very finely
   shredded and chopped

50g carrot, very finely grated

3 spring onions, finely chopped

75g strained kimchi, very finely
   chopped

sea salt and black pepper (optional)

**Dipping sauce**

2 tbsp soy sauce

1 tbsp rice wine vinegar

1 tbsp chilli oil (or to taste)

1 tsp sesame oil

**To cook**

vegetable oil

# Potstickers

Potsticker is the western name for these traditional Chinese dumplings, which are part-fried, part-steamed, so the bottoms are fabulously sticky and gorgeous and the tops tender and soft. You can buy the wrappers, usually labelled gyoza wrappers, in Asian supermarkets but if you feel like tackling them yourself, have a look at our recipe on page 267. One word of advice, do be sure to shred the cabbage and carrot very finely and then cut any long strands up again. Otherwise you will find that the pieces will be hard to fit on a teaspoon when you're filling the dumplings.

---

Heat the oil in a frying pan and gently cook the Chinese cabbage, carrot and spring onions until they have wilted down. Remove from the heat and stir in the kimchi. Taste for seasoning and add salt and pepper if you think it necessary. Allow to cool.

Assemble the dumplings by putting a teaspoon of filling in the centre of each wrapper. Wet around the sides – thoroughly, as they can sometimes crack – then pinch the edges together, pleating from the middle down each side to seal.

Make the dipping sauce by mixing everything together. Taste for seasoning and add salt if necessary.

To cook, heat some vegetable oil in a non-stick frying pan that has a lid – you need just enough oil to thinly cover the base. Add some of the dumplings, making sure they are well spread out.

Fry the dumplings over a medium heat until they are crisp and brown underneath, then add water – just enough to thinly cover the base of the pan. Cover the pan quickly, as it will spit when you add the water, and steam the dumplings for 5 minutes, until they are starting to look translucent and the water has evaporated. Uncover and cook for a further minute to make sure the underside is still crisp. Remove and keep warm while you cook the rest. Serve hot with the dipping sauce.

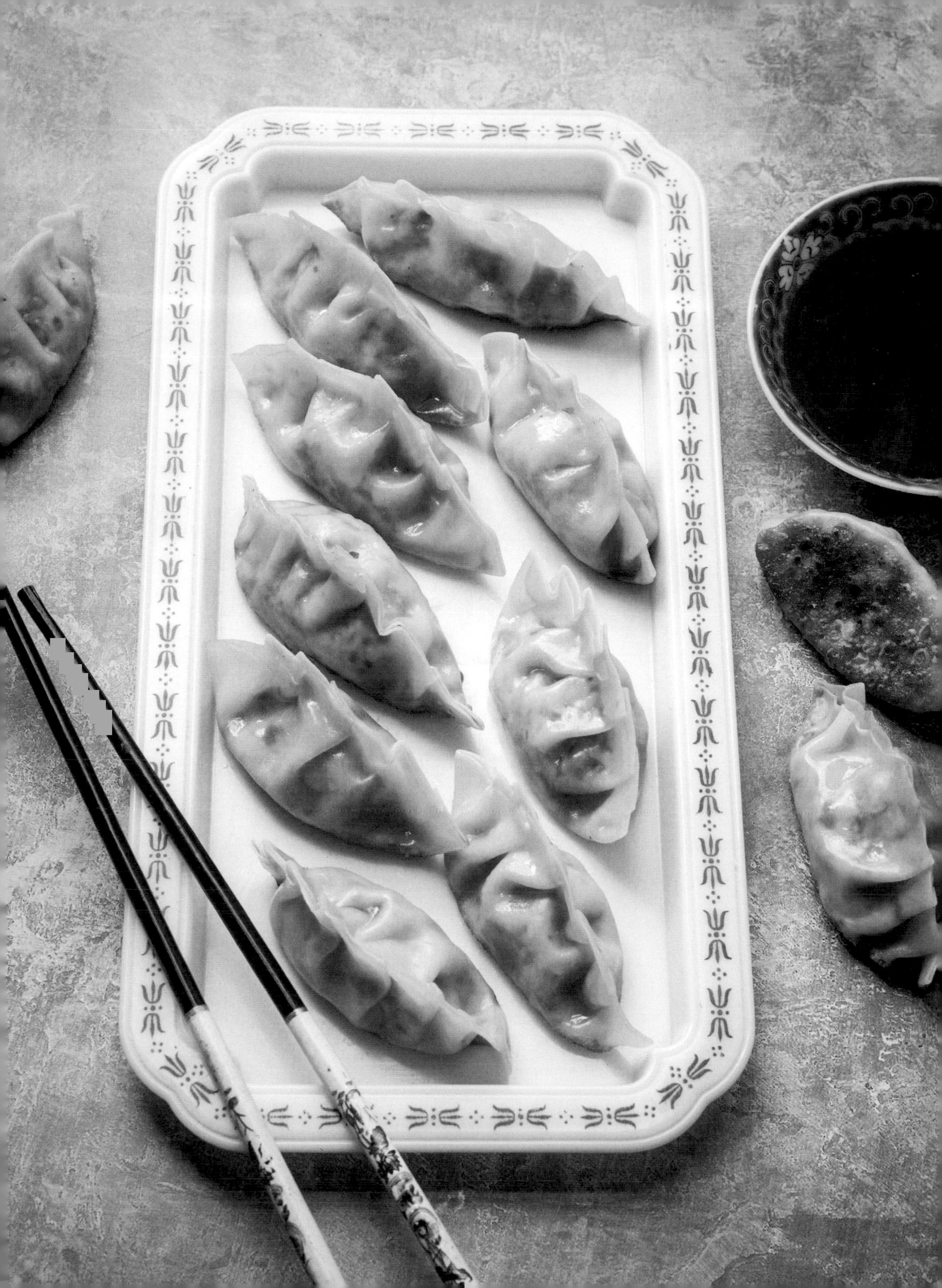

125g artichoke hearts (from a jar, preferably in oil not brine)

125g vegetarian cream cheese or quark

75g vegetarian hard cheese, grated

zest of 1 lemon

juice of ½ lemon

1 tsp white wine vinegar

handful of basil leaves

pinch of sugar

sea salt and black pepper

# Artichoke & basil dip

**A super-quick dip, using the chargrilled artichoke hearts you can find on deli counters and in jars.**

Put everything in a food processor and season with plenty of salt and pepper. Whizz until you have a fairly smooth, green-flecked purée. Taste for seasoning and adjust with more salt, pepper, lemon juice or sugar as necessary. Tip into a bowl and serve with sticks of raw veg, crackers or whatever you fancy.

SERVES 4

2 red peppers, cut in half and deseeded, or 150g roasted peppers from a jar

400g can of chickpeas, drained

1 garlic clove, crushed

zest of 1 lemon

1 tbsp lemon juice

generous pinch of ground turmeric

½ tsp ground cinnamon

3 tbsp olive oil

½ tsp chilli flakes, plus extra for sprinkling

pinch of za'atar

sea salt and black pepper

# Red pepper hummus

**For this you can roast your own peppers and skin them, as below, or buy them ready roasted and peeled in a jar. Depends on how much time you have but either way, this is good.**

If roasting the red peppers, preheat the oven to 200°C/Fan 180°C/Gas 6. Place the peppers, cut-side down, on a roasting tin and roast for 30 minutes until the skins are blistered and blackened in patches. Remove the peppers from the oven and put them in a bowl. Cover with a plate and leave to steam while they cool. When they are cool enough to handle, peel off the skins.

Put the peppers in a food processor with all but 2 tablespoons of the chickpeas, the garlic, lemon zest and juice, turmeric and cinnamon. Season with plenty of salt and pepper. Blitz to make a smooth paste, then drizzle with 2 tablespoons of the olive oil. Scrape into a bowl.

Lightly crush the remaining chickpeas in a small bowl and season with salt, pepper and chilli flakes. Make a swirl in the hummus and drizzle over the remaining olive oil. Sprinkle over the crushed chickpeas and top with more chilli flakes and the za'atar and serve with sticks of raw veg, flatbreads or crackers.

2 x 200g rounds of tempeh
2 tbsp cornflour
1 tsp ground cumin
½ tsp hot chilli powder
½ tsp ground cinnamon
2 tbsp maple syrup

**Glaze**
2 tbsp maple syrup
1 tbsp ketchup
1 tsp hot chilli sauce
2 tbsp vegetable oil
sea salt and black pepper

**Garlic sauce**
200ml plant-based yoghurt
1 tbsp tahini
1 tbsp lemon juice
4 garlic cloves, crushed
½ tsp dried mint
½ tsp caster sugar

**To serve**
large flatbreads (the fluffy sort)
pickled chillies
wedges of iceberg lettuce
slices of cucumber, tomato, red onion
chilli sauce

# Tempeh shawarma

**Another bit of fusion here. Inspired by *Bake Off*'s Nadiya Hussein's chicken shawarma, we've taken that much-loved Middle Eastern dish and reinvented it with some Asian tempeh. Once the pieces of tempeh are built up in the tin and baked, you can slice it in the same way as a shawarma, and the glaze introduces all sorts of great flavour. Thank you, Nadiya.**

Preheat the oven to 200°C/Fan 180°C/Gas 6. Line a small loaf tin with some baking paper or foil. Mix all the glaze ingredients together and season with salt and pepper. Brush some of this over the base and sides of the lined tin.

Cut each round of tempeh into large irregular chunks (6–8 pieces per round), then cut each chunk into slices about ½cm thick.

Mix the cornflour with the spices and plenty of salt and pepper, then mix with 2 tablespoons of water. Add the maple syrup.

Brush the slices of tempeh with the cornflour mixture and arrange them in the tin, trying to leave as few gaps or holes as possible – a bit like making a dry stone wall. Brush over a little more glaze, then cover with oiled foil and weigh down with tins for half an hour.

Make the garlic sauce by mixing everything together and seasoning with salt and pepper.

Bake the tempeh in the oven for 20 minutes, then uncover and brush with more glaze. Bake for another 10–15 minutes until the top looks crisp and browned round the edges. Turn out and brush any remaining glaze over the bottom and sides.

Slice the tempeh very carefully into 1cm slices – it should resemble slices of chicken shawarma. Eat with flatbreads and any or all of our serving suggestions, plus lots of garlic sauce.

SERVES 4

1 tbsp olive oil
200g whole almonds
3 tbsp tamari
½ tsp smoked chilli powder
a few drops of sesame oil
sea salt

# Tamari almonds

**Ideal for serving with drinks or whenever you fancy a little something. Use almonds with their skins or blanched almonds, whichever you like.**

Heat the oil in a frying pan large enough to hold the almonds in a single layer. Add the almonds and toast them over a low to medium heat for 10–15 minutes, stirring regularly, until they start to brown and their nutty aroma has intensified.

Pour over the tamari and turn down the heat to its lowest setting. Stir the almonds until they are glossy and sticky with the tamari and all the liquid has evaporated from the pan. Keep frying until the nuts become less tacky. Remove from the heat and sprinkle with chilli powder, sesame oil and salt, then leave to cool.

SERVES 4

finely grated zest of 1 lemon
2 x 400g cans of chickpeas, drained
(or cook your own, see p.270)
1 tbsp olive oil
½ tsp dried oregano
½ tsp sea salt
½ tsp chilli powder

# Roasted chickpeas

**These are easy to make and so good. They're best with the larger chickpeas and it helps to rub off any loose skins.**

Preheat the oven to 200°C/Fan 180°C/Gas 6. While it is heating up, put the lemon zest on a tray and put it in the oven for a few minutes to dry out. Remove and set aside to cool.

Dry the chickpeas as well as possible on kitchen paper. Put them on a baking tray, stir in the oil to coat and roast them in the oven for up to 30 minutes. Start checking after 20 minutes – the chickpeas should be browned, crisp on the outside and still slightly soft in the centre. Don't worry if a few of them have split.

Remove from the oven and leave to cool. Grind the lemon zest with the oregano and salt with a pestle and mortar, then mix with the chilli powder. Sprinkle this over the chickpeas and mix well. These will keep for a few days in an airtight container.

# Potato skin crisps

SERVES 4

**Who doesn't love a crisp? Instead of throwing those potato peelings away, do yourself a favour and make these. You can deep-fry them in hot oil at 180°C if you prefer.**

enough potato peelings to fill a
    baking tray (see method)

1 tbsp olive oil

dried herbs, to taste

sea salt and black pepper

Preheat the oven to 200°C/Fan 180°C/Gas 6. Make sure the potatoes you are using are clean and dry. Check them over for any blemishes or bruises and cut them out. Peel the potatoes with a peeler – don't remove too much flesh with the skin as it will make it harder for them to crisp up. Try to peel the potatoes in long strips, about 2.5cm wide.

Toss the potato skins in the olive oil and season with salt. Spread them out on a baking tray in an even layer. Bake in the preheated oven for about 10 minutes until well browned and very crisp. Remove from the oven and drain on kitchen paper. Check for seasoning and add pepper and any dried herbs you like.

# Padron pepper tempura

SERVES 4

**Super-quick to make. Get your ingredients ready, then make the batter while the oil is heating up and you're good to go.**

250g padron peppers

flour, for dusting

vegetable oil, for deep-frying

**Batter**

250ml sparkling water, chilled

1 egg, broken up with chopsticks

110g plain flour

1 tbsp cornflour

sea salt

Get all your ingredients together and dust the padron peppers with flour. Half-fill a large saucepan or deep-fat fryer with oil and heat to about 180°C. Do not leave the pan unattended.

When the oil is just about ready, make the batter. Add the water to the egg, give it a very quick mix, then add the plain flour, cornflour and a generous pinch of salt. Do not whisk, just mix very briefly with chopsticks. There will be lumps but that's fine.

Dip the padron peppers in the batter – the flour should help it stick – and drop them into the heated oil a few at a time. Flip them over after about 30 seconds or when the underside is golden brown and continue cooking for another 30 seconds. Drain on kitchen paper, then sprinkle with salt and serve.

500g strong white flour
  (bread flour), plus extra
  for dusting

7g instant dried yeast
2 tsp caster sugar
2 tsp fine sea salt
250ml warm water
25g butter, at room temperature
50ml whole milk

**To boil**

3 tbsp bicarbonate of soda

**To top**

1 egg yolk
sesame seeds
poppy seeds
sea salt

# Dave's special pretzels

**An ideal snack with a cold beer, pretzels are low in fat and sugar – and so good to eat.**

First make the dough. Put the flour in a large bowl or in a stand mixer and add the yeast and sugar. Mix well, then add the salt. Measure the water into a jug and add the butter – the heat from the water should melt it. Add the milk and whisk to combine.

Work the liquids into the dry ingredients until you have a sticky dough, then leave it to stand for 10 minutes. Next, either knead your dough using the dough hook on your stand mixer or turn it out on to a clean, lightly floured work surface and knead until the dough is smooth and elastic.

Cover the dough with a damp tea towel and leave it somewhere warm until it has doubled in size. This will take at least an hour. Line 3 baking trays with baking paper and dust them generously with flour.

Turn the dough out and cut it into 12 even pieces. Roll each piece of dough into a long sausage, about 1cm in diameter and 50–60cm long. To shape into a classic pretzel, make a U shape with the roll, with the curve at the bottom. Take the 2 ends and twist them twice, then press the ends into the curve of the U. Gently shape them with your hands so they look roughly heart shaped. Whisk the egg yolk with 2 tablespoons of water and use a little to glue the ends on to the dough. Set aside the rest for glazing the pretzels later.

Roll and shape the remaining pieces of dough in the same way and place them on the baking trays. Leave to stand, uncovered, for half an hour. A 'skin' will form on the dough which will help with the texture. Preheat the oven to 210°C/ Fan 190°C /Gas 6½.

Pour a litre of just-boiled water into a large saucepan, making sure the pan is no more than half full. Bring back to a rolling boil and add the bicarbonate of soda – be careful, it will foam up.

Very gently take a pretzel, drop it into the water and leave it for 5 seconds, then flip it over and leave for another 5 seconds. Remove the pretzel from the pan with a slotted spoon and put it back on the baking tray. Continue until you have given all the pretzels a bath.

Glaze the pretzels with the egg yolk and water mix, then sprinkle generously with sesame seeds, poppy seeds or salt. Bake in the oven for 15–20 minutes, until they are a deep, glossy brown. Remove from the oven and leave to cool before eating.

**Pickled onions**

1 tsp granulated sugar

2 tsp salt

1 tsp chilli flakes

50ml cider or red wine vinegar

2 medium onions, finely sliced

**Batter**

70g gram (chickpea) flour

30g rice flour

1 tsp baking powder

1 tsp ground turmeric

1 tsp ground cumin

½ tsp ground cinnamon

15g fresh root ginger, grated

3 garlic cloves, crushed or grated

2 green chillies, finely chopped

2 tbsp finely chopped coriander
    stems

1 tbsp coconut oil, melted, or 1 tbsp
    plant-based coconut yoghurt

1 tbsp lemon juice

**To fry**

vegetable or groundnut oil

**To serve**

200ml plant-based yoghurt

50ml mango chutney

coriander leaves, finely chopped

# Pickled onion bhajis

Lancashire meets Lahore! We love pickled onions and we love bhajis – put the two together and you have a mega treat. Great with a cold beer. Gram flour is easy to find in supermarkets and the rice flour really helps get the batter beautifully crispy. If you don't have any, you can blitz rice to a powder in a spice grinder or a high-powered blender. And we suggest a nice little dip of yoghurt and mango chutney on the side for dipping. Obviously if you're not vegan, you can use ordinary plain yoghurt instead of plant-based.

---

First, pickle the onions. Mix the sugar, salt, chilli flakes and vinegar in a bowl. Stir until the sugar and salt has dissolved, then add the onions. Stir to coat and press them down into the vinegar, then top with just enough water to cover. Set aside for at least an hour, then drain thoroughly and dry on kitchen paper.

Just before you want to fry the bhajis, make the batter. Whisk all the ingredients together, then add just enough water to make the batter roughly the consistency of double cream. Stir in the onions.

Half-fill a large saucepan or deep-fat fryer with oil and heat it to about 180°C. Do not leave the pan unattended.

Take heaped tablespoons of the mixture and drop them into the oil. Fry the bhajis for 2–3 minutes on each side until they are a deep ochre brown, then drain on kitchen paper. Cook the bhajis a few at a time – do not overcrowd the pan or the temperature of the oil will drop, and they may go soggy as opposed to crisp.

Mix the yoghurt, mango chutney and coriander together in a bowl, and serve with the hot bhajis.

# Fab falafel

300g dried chickpeas, soaked overnight, then drained

zest and juice of 1 lemon

1 tsp ground cumin

1 tsp ground coriander

½ tsp ground cinnamon

½ tsp ground ginger

½ tsp ground allspice

1 tsp baking powder

1 tsp salt

1 preserved lemon, skin only, finely chopped

4 spring onions, finely chopped

4 garlic cloves, finely chopped

small bunch of parsley, roughly chopped

leaves from a large sprig of thyme

vegetable oil, for frying

**Tahini sauce**

100g tahini, well mixed

1 tbsp date or maple syrup

1 tsp salt

1 tsp garlic powder

juice of ½ lemon

100ml warm water

**To serve**

pitta or flatbreads, split and toasted

chilli sauce (optional)

lemon wedges

tomatoes, cucumber, lettuce, peppers, onions, pickled chillies

a few herbs (such as parsley, mint, coriander)

**Yes, we know you can buy falafel but wait until you try these. You'll be amazed at how tasty they are. And actually, it's not too much of a faff to make falafel. You just have to remember to soak the chickpeas the night before and the rest is easy. Serve them up with some pitta or flatbread and whatever salad bits and bobs you fancy. The tahini dip is great, but if you're not vegan you might like to have a yoghurt dip instead.**

Put half the chickpeas in a food processor with half the lemon zest and juice and pulse until fairly smooth. Scrape the mixture into a bowl. Process the remaining chickpeas with the rest of the zest and juice until broken down but still quite coarse, then add the other ingredients, except the oil. Process until everything is well broken down and combined. Add this to the bowl with the first batch of chickpeas and mix well by hand – a kneading action works well.

Divide the mixture into balls or patties weighing about 35g each. We find that small balls are best if you're deep-frying, but patties work well for shallow frying. You should get at least 20. Leave the falafel in the fridge to chill for half an hour before cooking.

Meanwhile, whisk the ingredients for the tahini sauce together until smooth. The consistency should be like thick, pourable double cream – thin it out with a little warm water if necessary. Gather together all the accompaniments.

To cook the falafel, half-fill a deep-fat fryer or a large saucepan with oil and heat to about 180°C. Add the falafel, a few at a time, and fry until deep brown. Remove with a slotted spoon and set aside to drain on kitchen paper while you fry the rest.

If you prefer, you can shallow fry the falafel. Cover the base of a frying pan with ½cm of oil and heat. Fry the falafel a few at a time, so you don't overcrowd the pan. They will take 4–5 minutes on each side over a medium-high heat. Drain on kitchen paper.

Serve the falafel piping hot with the tahini sauce, pitta or flat breads and other accompaniments.

MAKES 8

# Cheese, potato & onion pasties

## Pastry
450g plain flour, plus extra for dusting

2 tsp baking powder

1 tsp salt

125g cold butter, diced

1 egg yolk

up to 125ml iced water

1 egg, beaten, for sealing and brushing

## Filling
2 medium onions, finely diced

250g potatoes (peeled weight), finely diced

300g vegetarian Cheddar cheese or similar, grated

1 tsp mustard powder

sea salt and black pepper

**For us, a picnic isn't a picnic without a pasty. But you can enjoy these little beauties anywhere, indoors or out. Serve with the tomato relish on page 259 if you like. Bet you can't eat just one.**

First make the pastry. Put the flour, baking powder and salt into a food processor or stand mixer, add the butter and egg yolk and process until the mixture resembles fine breadcrumbs. Gradually work in the water until you have a smooth dough – you may only need about 100ml. Wrap the dough in cling film and chill for at least half an hour. You can make the pastry by hand if you prefer.

Mix the filling ingredients together and season. Preheat the oven to 180°C/Fan 160°C/Gas 4.

Divide your dough into 8 even pieces – weigh them to check. Roll out each piece on a floured work surface into a round of about 19cm – use a plate as a guide if you like. Don't worry if the pastry looks thin, the baking powder will ensure it thickens up in the oven.

Measure out an eighth of the filling and place it on one side of a disc of pastry. Make sure you have a 2cm border around it and squish it down slightly, so it is compacted. Brush around the edge of the disc with beaten egg.

Stretch the uncovered half of the pastry over and press down on to the border – it doesn't matter if the edges don't match up completely as you're going to crimp them. The traditional method is to put your finger just to the left of one end, then with the other hand lift up the end and twist the pastry over, moving your finger out of the way just before you press the pastry down. Continue all the way round and tuck the end under.

Continue until you have made 8 pasties. Place them on baking trays and bake for about 50 minutes, until the pastry is richly coloured. Remove the pasties from the oven and eat hot or cold.

SERVES 4

# BLT, vegan-style

This is a slightly different version of our tofu bacon and ideal for making a vegan version of our favourite sandwich – the BLT! Try to cut the tofu into nice long thin slices so it looks like bacon, then layer it up with the rest of the ingredients to make a truly brilliant feast.

---

**Tofu bacon**

400g smoked tofu

1 tbsp maple syrup

2 tbsp soy sauce

a dash of hot sauce

½ tsp garlic powder

1 tsp onion granules

½ tsp annatto powder or
    ½ tsp mild chilli powder

a few drops of liquid smoke
    or ½ tsp smoked salt

1 tsp dried mixed herbs

2 tbsp olive oil

**Sandwiches**

2 tbsp vegan mayonnaise

1 tbsp Dijon mustard

8 slices of bread

1 little gem lettuce or similar,
    leaves left whole

1 red onion, very thinly sliced
    into rounds

4 medium tomatoes, sliced
    into rounds

2 large avocados, pitted and sliced

squeeze of lime juice

sea salt

**Optional extras**

1 tbsp vegan kimchi or sauerkraut
    per sandwich, well drained

large gherkins, sliced

pickled jalapeños

Cut the tofu into thin slices like rashers of streaky bacon – you should get at least 24. Whisk all the remaining bacon tofu ingredients, except the oil, together to make the glaze.

You will probably have to fry the tofu in a couple of batches, so heat half the oil in a large frying pan, then brush one side of each slice of tofu with the glaze.

Fry the slices, glaze-side down, and while they are frying, glaze the top sides. When the tofu slices are a deep ochre brown on the underside and crisp round the edges, fry them on the other side. Repeat until you have used up all the tofu, then drain on kitchen paper.

To assemble the sandwiches, mix the mayonnaise and mustard together and spread it over one side of each slice of bread. Add the bacon tofu, lettuce, red onion and tomato in layers, dividing them between 4 slices of bread. Season the avocado with salt and lime juice and add it too, along with any of the optional extras. Top with the remaining slices of bread and cut each sandwich in half to serve.

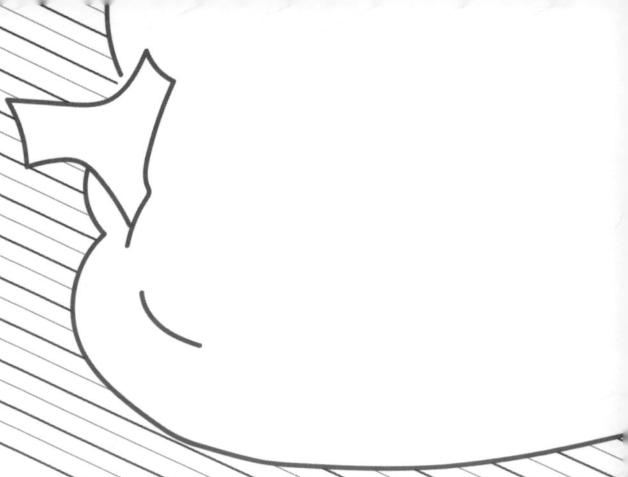

Brussels sprout & chestnut barley risotto 124

Tempeh rendang 126

Couscous-stuffed peppers 128

Spaghetti & 'meatballs' 130

Sweet & sour tofu 132

Pasta with creamy black pepper sauce 134

Root vegetable tray bake 136

Stuffed baked potatoes 138

Chow mein 140

Roast cauliflower steaks 142

Keema peas with paneer 144

Quick jackfruit korma 146

Vegan plate pie 148

Roasted aubergine pasta 150

Mediterranean-style vegetable bake 152

Fennel & turnip tagine 154

Chilli bean bake 156

Succotash 158

SERVES 4 ⊘

# Brussels sprout & chestnut barley risotto

1.5 litres well-flavoured vegetable stock

200g cooked chestnuts

3 large sprigs of sage

1 bay leaf

2 tbsp olive oil

50g butter

1 large onion, finely chopped

2 garlic cloves, finely chopped

250g pearl barley

100ml white wine

50g vegetarian Parmesan-style cheese, grated

400g Brussels sprouts, halved or quartered, depending on size

sea salt and black pepper

There's a nice festive vibe to this risotto featuring two classic Christmas dinner ingredients – sprouts and chestnuts – and the barley gives it a robust touch that makes it an ideal meal for a winter's night. Vac-packed chestnuts work fine, and you can use frozen sprouts if you like.

Put the stock in a saucepan. Put half the chestnuts in a food processor or blender, add a ladleful of stock and blitz to a purée. Set aside. Bruise 2 sprigs of sage and add them and the bay leaf to the stock. Bring the stock to the boil, then remove from the heat.

Heat a tablespoon of the oil in a large sauté pan and add half the butter. When it is foaming, add the onion and cook gently until soft and translucent. Add the garlic and barley and stir until the barley is glossy. Season with salt and pepper.

Reheat the stock and keep it warm over a very low heat. Pour the wine into the pan with the barley and bring it to the boil. When the wine has boiled off, add the chestnut purée and a ladleful of stock. Stir, then bring to the boil, stirring regularly. When most of the stock has been absorbed, add another ladleful. Keep adding stock, allowing each addition to be absorbed before adding another, until the barley is tender and the sauce around it is creamy. You may not need all of the stock. Beat in the remaining butter and the cheese. Keep warm.

Blanch the sprouts in a saucepan of boiling water for 2 minutes, then drain well. Heat the remaining oil in a frying pan and add the sprouts. Fry, stirring regularly, until they are browned on the cut edges but still a vibrant green. Roughly chop the remaining chestnuts, add them to the pan and cook for another couple of minutes. Finely chop the remaining sage and toss with the sprouts and chestnuts.

Serve the risotto with half the sprouts and chestnuts stirred through, then add the rest as a garnish.

**Paste**

3 shallots, roughly chopped

2 lemongrass stalks, white centres
  only, roughly chopped

25g fresh root ginger,
  roughly chopped

4 garlic cloves, roughly chopped

2 red chillies, roughly chopped

½ tsp black peppercorns

1 tsp ground turmeric

**Rendang**

1 tbsp coconut oil

5cm piece of cinnamon stick

4 cloves

1 star anise

5 cardamom pods

400ml can of coconut milk

2 tbsp soy sauce

2 tsp tamarind paste

1 tbsp palm sugar or
  light soft brown sugar

300g salad potatoes,
  cut into ½cm slices

300g tempeh, roughly chopped

8 lime leaves, very finely sliced

**Garnish**

30g desiccated coconut

coriander leaves

# Tempeh rendang

Rendang is an Indonesian dish, usually made with meat, but we've used tempeh for this vegan version. As it happens, tempeh also originates from Indonesia – it's made from cooked soya beans which are fermented and made into patties. It's a great source of protein and soaks up other flavours brilliantly, so works really well here.

First make the paste. Put everything in a small food processor and pulse until you have a smooth paste. Add a little water if it is initially reluctant to break down.

For the rendang, heat the oil in a large pan or a flameproof casserole dish. Add the paste and all the spices, then fry them in the oil until it starts to smell intensely aromatic. Add the coconut milk, soy sauce, tamarind paste and sugar along with 100ml of water and stir until the sugar is dissolved. Bring to the boil, then add the potatoes and cover the pan. Simmer for 15 minutes or until the potatoes are tender.

Add the tempeh to the pan and continue to simmer, this time uncovered, until the sauce is well reduced.

Make the garnish. Put the coconut into a dry frying pan and toast, stirring regularly, until golden brown. Remove from the heat and leave to cool, then grind to form a coarse powder.

Serve the rendang garnished with the coconut and coriander leaves. Good with roti or rice.

# Couscous-stuffed peppers

4 peppers, deseeded and cut in half lengthways

sea salt and black pepper

**Stuffing**

75g giant couscous

2 tbsp olive oil

1 medium red onion, very finely chopped

1 courgette (about 200g) finely diced

2 garlic cloves, finely chopped

100g chargrilled artichokes (from a jar), diced

1 tsp ground cinnamon

1 tsp dried mint

small bunch of parsley, finely chopped

100g cherry tomatoes, quartered

juice of 1 lemon

**Topping**

1 tbsp olive oil

50g breadcrumbs

25g pine nuts

2 tbsp finely chopped parsley

zest of 1 lemon

A veggie classic, but we think ours are just that bit nicer than the usual. Stuffed peppers are often topped with cheese, but we wanted to make a tasty vegan version and we think this breadcrumb and pine nut topping is crunchy and delicious. Giant couscous has a bit more oomph and texture than the regular sort and works well for the stuffing. You can buy it in most supermarkets.

Preheat the oven to 200°C/Fan 180°C/Gas 6. Arrange the red peppers in an ovenproof dish, large enough to hold them all in one layer, then season with salt and pepper. Add 100ml of water to the dish – this will create steam and help the peppers soften. Bake them in the oven for about 20 minutes until they start to soften, then remove and leave to cool a little.

Meanwhile, make the filling. Put the couscous in a saucepan with 200ml of water. Bring to the boil, then turn the heat down and cover the pan. Cook until the couscous is just tender and all the water has been absorbed.

Heat the oil in a frying pan and add the onion and courgette. Cook until the onion is translucent and the courgette is starting to brown, then add the garlic. Cook for a further minute, then add the artichokes, cinnamon and mint. Season generously with salt and pepper, then remove from the heat and leave to cool for a while. Add the parsley, cherry tomatoes, lemon juice and cooked couscous. Taste again, and add more seasoning, cinnamon and mint if necessary.

Pile the stuffing into the peppers. For the topping, put the olive oil in a bowl and mix in the breadcrumbs, pine nuts, parsley and lemon zest. Season with salt and pepper, then sprinkle the mixture over the peppers. Put them back in the oven for 10–15 minutes until the tops are golden brown. The peppers should be just on the soft side of al dente. Serve with salad leaves.

SERVES 4

# Spaghetti & 'meatballs'

The aubergine in these 'meatballs' gives them a good robust texture and they're packed with flavour too. Who needs meat? You can make the balls and the tomato sauce in advance, if you like, then supper is dead easy to put together. This makes a great family supper dish.

**'Meatballs'**

3 tbsp olive oil

1 medium onion, very finely chopped

2 large aubergines, very finely diced

3 garlic cloves, crushed or grated

2 tsp dried oregano

1 tbsp tapenade

75g fresh breadcrumbs

50g vegetarian hard cheese, finely grated

25g pine nuts, toasted and finely chopped

1 tsp sweet smoked paprika

25g parsley, finely chopped

1 egg, beaten

sea salt and black pepper

**To serve**

500g spaghetti or linguini

½ portion of tomato sauce (see p.263)

sprigs of basil

vegetarian hard cheese, grated

First make the balls. Heat the oil in a large frying pan and add the onion and diced aubergines. Cook over a medium-high heat until both are nicely browned, then add the garlic, oregano, tapenade and plenty of salt and pepper. Cook for another couple of minutes. Remove from the heat and leave to cool down.

Put the breadcrumbs, cheese and nuts into a large bowl. Sprinkle in the paprika and parsley and season with salt and pepper. Add the aubergine mixture and the egg and stir to combine, then put the mixture in the fridge to chill for half an hour.

Preheat the oven to 200°C/Fan 180°C/Gas 6. Shape the mixture into balls slightly smaller than a golf ball – about 30g each. You should end up with 20. Arrange them on a baking tray and bake for 20 minutes until crisp and brown.

Cook the pasta in plenty of salted water. While the pasta is cooking, warm through the tomato sauce and add the balls to it. Heat them through, then serve with the pasta. Garnish with a few sprigs of basil and plenty of grated cheese.

SERVES 4

# Sweet & sour tofu

There's nothing like a good old sweet and sour and this vegan version is quick to cook once you've prepared all the ingredients. If you have extra-firm tofu it shouldn't need pressing for this, but if you're using firm tofu, press it as in the recipe on page 20. Who needs a carry-out?

---

**Sauce**

1 tbsp soy sauce

2 tbsp Chinese vinegar

1 tbsp light soft brown sugar

1 tbsp sweet chilli sauce

100ml pineapple juice

½ tsp Chinese 5-spice

1 tsp cornflour

sea salt and black pepper

**Tofu**

1 x 280–300g block of extra-firm tofu, cut into chunks

2 tsp cornflour

½ tsp garlic powder

1 tbsp vegetable oil

**Vegetables**

200g broccoli florets

1 tbsp vegetable oil

1 large onion, cut into chunks (cut into thick wedges and cut each wedge into thirds)

1 red pepper, deseeded and cut into chunks

1 green pepper, deseeded and cut into chunks

2 garlic cloves, finely chopped

25g fresh root ginger, finely chopped

150g canned pineapple in fruit juice, cut into chunks

**To serve**

1 tsp sesame oil

1 tsp sesame seeds

a few sprigs of coriander

First make the sauce by whisking all the ingredients together until the sugar has dissolved. Season with salt and pepper.

Next fry the tofu. Make sure the tofu is very dry, then toss it in the cornflour and garlic powder. Heat the oil in a wok or a large frying pan. When the air above it is shimmering, add the tofu and fry on all sides until crisp and golden brown. Remove from the wok and set aside.

Blanch the broccoli in boiling salted water until tender, then drain and refresh in a bowl of iced water or run it under a cold tap. Drain again and set aside.

Add more oil to the wok or frying pan and stir-fry the onion, peppers and broccoli together for a few minutes or until just al dente – they need to have some bite. Add the garlic and ginger and cook for a further 2 minutes, then pour in the sauce ingredients and the pineapple.

Simmer until the sauce starts to thicken a little, then return the tofu to the pan. Drizzle over a teaspoon of sesame oil and sprinkle with sesame seeds and coriander. Serve with some rice, if you like.

SERVES 4

# Pasta with creamy black pepper sauce

75g unsalted cashew nuts

75g butternut squash, diced

125ml plant-based milk
(oat, soya or almond)

½ tsp garlic powder

½ tsp Marmite

1 tbsp olive oil

1 small onion, very finely chopped

1 bay leaf

2 garlic cloves, very finely chopped

1 tbsp black peppercorns,
coarsely ground

½ tsp maple syrup (optional)

grating of nutmeg

sea salt and black pepper

**To serve**

400g tagliatelle pasta (check it is
egg-free)

100g spinach or rocket (optional)

shavings of vegan Parmesan-style
cheese (optional)

The creamy pasta dish known as pasta alfredo is a great favourite of ours, and Dave is a massive fan of another simple classic – cacio e pepe, which is pasta served with cheese and black pepper. We thought it would be fun to make a sort of mixture of the two as a vegan recipe and this is it. Try it – we think it's something special.

Put the cashew nuts and butternut squash in a pan and cover with water. Bring to the boil, then simmer until the cashew nuts are soft. This will take about 15 minutes. Drain and put the nuts and squash in a blender with the milk, garlic powder and Marmite. Blitz until you have a completely smooth sauce.

Heat the oil in a frying pan and add the onion and bay leaf. Cook gently until the onion is completely soft and translucent, then add the garlic and black peppercorns. Continue to cook for a few more minutes, then add the sauce. Season with salt and stir to combine. Taste and add the maple syrup if you would like a slightly sweeter sauce, then grate in a few rasps of nutmeg.

While the onion is cooking, bring a large saucepan of water to the boil and add plenty of salt. Cook the pasta until it is al dente, then add the spinach or rocket, if using. As soon as the leaves have wilted, scoop 2 ladlefuls of the pasta water into a jug, then drain the pasta.

Toss the pasta in the sauce, adding some of the pasta water if it is too thick. Serve immediately with plenty of black pepper and shavings of vegan cheese, if using.

# Root vegetable tray bake

300g carrots, left whole if slender enough, or cut lengthways

300g beetroots, cut into wedges

300g celeriac, cut into wedges

2 tbsp olive oil

2 red onions, cut into wedges

a few sprigs of thyme

400g can of cannellini beans, drained

sea salt and black pepper

**Sage & onion balls**

1 tbsp olive oil

15g butter

1 large onion, finely chopped

1 tsp dried sage, crumbled

zest of 1 lemon

150g breadcrumbs

1 egg, beaten

**Sauce**

150ml cider

1 tsp Dijon mustard

1 tsp redcurrant or apple or herb jelly

1 tsp Marmite

150ml vegetable stock, heated

A tray bake like this is a great way to enjoy lots of lovely root veg. This one is topped with some delicious little sage and onion balls and a sticky flavoursome sauce. The three component parts make a complete satisfying meal – just the sort of thing we wanted for this book.

Preheat the oven to 200°C/Fan 180°C/Gas 6. Arrange the carrots, beetroots and celeriac in a large roasting tin and drizzle with a tablespoon of the oil. Season with salt and pepper, then roast for 20 minutes. Remove from the oven. Toss the onion wedges in the remaining oil and season with salt, then add the onions and thyme to the tin and put it back in the oven for another 20 minutes.

Meanwhile, make the sage and onion balls. Heat the oil and butter in a frying pan, add the chopped onion and cook until soft and translucent. Add the sage and lemon zest, then remove the frying pan from the heat. Tip the mixture into a bowl and add the breadcrumbs, then season well and stir in the egg. Form the mixture into 8 balls.

Whisk the sauce ingredients together and set aside.

Remove the roasting tin from the oven and sprinkle the beans over the veg. Pour over the sauce. Arrange the balls on top, then roast for another 15–20 minutes until the balls are cooked through and browned and the sauce has reduced – it should be syrupy and should have formed a sticky glaze on the top of the vegetables. Serve with something green, perhaps a large bowl of peas.

4 large baking potatoes
1 tbsp olive oil
sea salt and black pepper

**Leek and blue cheese filling**
1 tbsp olive oil
15g butter, plus extra for dotting
    on top
4 leeks, sliced
100ml vermouth or white wine
100g vegetarian blue cheese, diced
25g walnuts, finely chopped

# Stuffed baked potatoes

We reckon that one of the all-time most comforting meals is a baked potato. It's great just as it is, slathered with butter and topped with grated cheese, but even better with our leek and blue cheese filling.

---

Preheat the oven to 180°C/Fan 160°C/Gas 4. Pierce the potatoes all over with a fork or skewer, then rub them with olive oil and season with salt. Place them directly on the oven shelf and bake for 60–70 minutes until tender all the way through.

To make the leek and blue cheese filling, heat the oil and 15g of butter in a large frying or sauté pan with a lid. Add the leeks and cook them gently over a medium heat for several minutes until they are starting to soften and look glossy with butter – don't let them brown. Add the vermouth or white wine and bring to the boil. Leave to bubble until the liquid has reduced by half, then lower the heat. Cover the pan, and leave to simmer until the leeks are tender, then tip them into a bowl and set aside.

When the baked potatoes are done, take them out of the oven and cut them in half. Scoop out the flesh and break it up – don't mash, just crush it a little. Add the potato and blue cheese to the leeks, season with salt and pepper and stir together.

Spoon the mixture into the potato skins. Sprinkle with the walnuts, then dot with a little more butter. Put them back in the oven and bake for 10–15 minutes until lightly browned.

> **✓ BIKER VEGAN TIP**
>
> For a vegan feast, top your tatties with some home-made vegan baked beans (see p.253).

SERVES 4

15g dried shiitake mushrooms

1 tbsp soy sauce

1 tsp sugar

1 tbsp mirin, Chinese rice wine or Shaoxing wine

250g dried noodles (check they are egg-free)

1 tsp sesame oil

1 tbsp vegetable oil

½ Chinese cabbage, very finely shredded

2 large carrots, cut into matchsticks

2 garlic cloves, finely chopped

15g fresh root ginger, finely chopped

100g bean sprouts

4 spring onions, finely sliced

**To serve**

chilli sauce

sesame oil

# Chow mein

A regular chow mein is usually made with oyster sauce, but using dried mushrooms gives a similar lovely umami flavour. We like cabbage and carrots in this recipe, but you can add more veg if you like – it's a great way of using up any odds and ends in the fridge. Cut the veg into slender shapes similar to the noodles and, if you are making this as a vegan dish, check that the noodles you're using aren't made with egg. Lovely served with the sweet and sour tofu on page 132.

Soak the dried mushrooms in warm water for 30 minutes, then drain, reserving the soaking liquid. Mix the soy sauce, sugar and mirin, rice wine or Shaoxing wine together and add 2 tablespoons of the mushroom soaking liquid. Set aside.

Cook the noodles according to the packet instructions, then refresh them under cold water. Toss them in the sesame oil to keep them from clumping together.

Chop the soaked mushrooms very finely. Heat the vegetable oil in a wok or large frying pan and add the cabbage and carrots. Stir-fry until the carrots are soft, then add the garlic, ginger, bean sprouts and finely chopped mushrooms. Continue to cook for a couple of minutes.

Add the noodles to the vegetables and fry for another 2 minutes. Pour over the soy sauce mixture and continue to stir-fry until everything is well combined.

Sprinkle with the spring onions and serve immediately, with chilli sauce and sesame oil to add at the table.

SERVES 4

# Roast cauliflower steaks

**Couscous**

150g wholemeal couscous

1 tsp dried oregano

juice and zest of 1 orange

2 tbsp olive oil

150ml tepid water

large pinch of saffron

50g golden sultanas or raisins

small bunches of dill, mint,
coriander and parsley

1 small red onion, very finely diced

30g pumpkin seeds

25g pistachio nibs (or whole
pistachios cut into slivers)

1 orange, peel cut away and
flesh diced

sea salt and black pepper

**Cauliflower steaks**

2 large cauliflowers

2 tbsp olive oil

juice of ½ lemon

2 tbsp za'atar

**Salad dressing**

1 tbsp olive oil

1 tbsp sherry vinegar

1 tbsp orange juice (can be squeezed
from the discarded orange peel)

1 tbsp lemon juice

1 tbsp saffron soaking liquid

**To serve**

salad leaves

Cauliflower is great value and chunky slices of cauli make a good centrepiece for a meal. You'll only use the big centre sections for this, so save the rest for something else, such as cauliflower rice (see page 256). The steaks are excellent served with this flavourful couscous salad. Za'atar is a spice mix, available in supermarkets.

Put the couscous in a bowl with the oregano, orange juice and zest, plenty of seasoning and the oil. Pour over the water, then cover the bowl with a plate and leave the couscous to stand until all the liquid has been absorbed. Put the saffron into a mortar with a pinch of salt and grind to form a powder. Put this in a bowl with the sultanas or raisins and add just enough freshly boiled water to cover. Leave to stand for half an hour.

Preheat the oven to 200°C/Fan 180°C/Gas 6. Prepare the cauliflowers. Cut each one in half then cut one 'steak', about 2cm thick, from each half, giving you 4 'steaks'.

Heat the oil in a frying pan and sear the steaks for a couple of minutes on each side. You may have to do this in 2 batches. Arrange them on a baking tray, then drizzle with the lemon juice, season and sprinkle over the za'atar. Roast the slices for about 10 minutes until tender all the way through when pierced with the point of a knife

Meanwhile, finish the couscous. Tear the leaves off the bunches of herbs if very large (don't cut them) and mix most of them into the couscous, leaving the rest for the garnish. Mix in the onion and half each of the pumpkin seeds, pistachios and diced orange. Drain the sultanas or raisins, reserving a tablespoon of the soaking liquor for the dressing, and add half of them to the couscous.

To serve, arrange the couscous and salad leaves over 4 plates. Whisk the dressing ingredients together and drizzle it over the salad, then add the cauliflower steaks. Garnish with the remaining herbs, pumpkin seeds, nuts, diced orange and sultanas or raisins.

# Keema peas with paneer

SERVES 4

We've made this dish for years with minced lamb, often adding some lentils as well. Here is our new version with Quorn which we think is great. Lovely with some flatbread to scoop up the delicious peas. We like to serve the keema peas and the paneer separately, as we enjoy the crispy texture of the cheese with the silky peas, but you can mix it all together if you prefer.

---

**Keema peas**

2 tbsp coconut oil

1 onion, finely chopped

25g fresh root ginger, grated or finely chopped

3 garlic cloves, crushed or finely chopped

1 tsp mustard seeds

1–2 tbsp Biker spice mix (see p.266) or curry powder

2 tbsp coriander stems, finely chopped

150g Quorn mince

150g cooked brown lentils

200ml coconut milk

200g canned tomatoes

300g frozen peas

lemon juice (optional)

sea salt and black pepper

**Paneer**

juice of ½ lemon

1 tsp ground coriander

½ tsp chilli powder

½ tsp ground turmeric

1 x 200–250g block of paneer, diced

1 tbsp coconut oil

1 tsp cumin seeds

**Garnish**

coriander leaves

green chillies, finely sliced

For the keema peas, heat the coconut oil in a large saucepan or a flameproof casserole dish. Add the onion and cook over a low to medium heat until soft and translucent. Add the ginger, garlic, mustard seeds and the spice mix or curry powder and stir for another couple of minutes.

Add the coriander stems, Quorn and lentils to the pan. Stir to combine, then pour in the coconut milk, tomatoes and 100ml of water. Season with salt, bring to the boil, then turn the heat down to a simmer. Put the peas in a bowl and pour over boiling water to defrost them, then drain and add them to the pan.

Partially cover the pan with a lid and leave to simmer for about 20 minutes. Taste and adjust the seasoning as necessary and add a squeeze of lemon juice if you like. Garnish with coriander leaves and sliced green chillies.

For the paneer, mix the lemon juice with the ground spices in a bowl and add half a teaspoon of salt. Toss the paneer in this mixture until all the pieces are well coated. Heat the oil in a frying pan and add the cumin seeds. When they begin to pop, add the paneer. Fry the pieces on each side until crisp on the outside, softer within, and a rich golden brown. Garnish with coriander and green chillies and serve with the keema peas.

 **BIKER VEGAN TIP**

If you'd like to make this recipe vegan, just swap the paneer for tofu. Get some firm or extra-firm tofu, pat it dry and prepare as for the paneer. The keema peas are vegan anyway.

SERVES 4

2 tbsp vegetable oil

1 onion, finely chopped

3 garlic cloves, roughly chopped

25g fresh root ginger, peeled and roughly chopped

½ tsp ground cinnamon

½ tsp ground cardamom

½ tsp ground turmeric

a pinch of cloves

2 bay leaves

1 small tomato, chopped

75g unsalted cashew nuts or almonds, ground

1 tsp caster sugar

400g can of jackfruit, drained

250g fresh spinach, well washed

100ml plant-based double cream or yoghurt

sea salt and black pepper

**To serve**

1 tbsp vegetable oil

10–12 curry leaves

½ tsp mustard seeds

a few sprigs of coriander

3–4 green chillies, finely sliced

rice or flatbreads

# Quick jackfruit korma

**This is a gentle curry with the beautiful creamy texture that we all love about a korma. Jackfruit is an Asian fruit that's become increasingly popular in vegan cooking for its uncannily meaty texture and its ability to absorb flavour. You can sometimes find fresh jackfruit in Asian shops, but we use canned – available in most supermarkets.**

First heat the oil in a large saucepan and add the onion. Fry over a medium heat until the onion has softened and lightly browned. Purée the garlic and ginger together in a food processor, adding a little water to help them break down. Add this to the onion with the spices, bay leaves and tomato. Season with salt and pepper and stir for 3–4 minutes.

Stir in the ground cashew nuts or almonds and the sugar and add 500ml of water. Stir to make sure the nuts are well distributed and not clumping together, then add the jackfruit. Bring to the boil, then turn the heat down and simmer, partially covered, for about 20 minutes to ensure the jackfruit absorbs the flavours.

Loosen the sauce with a little more water if necessary, then add the spinach to the pan. When it has wilted down, add the cream or yoghurt. Stir to combine and leave over a very gentle heat to make sure the sauce doesn't split.

Prepare the garnish. Heat the oil in a small pan over a medium heat and add the curry leaves and mustard seeds. When the seeds start popping and the leaves are crisp and crackling, remove the pan from the heat and pour the contents over the curry. Serve sprinkled with coriander and chillies with some rice or flatbread.

SERVES 4

# Vegan plate pie

We're northerners and we must have a plate pie once in a while, so we've come up with a deliciously veg-packed vegan version which we really enjoy. This is what Si calls a 'cut and come again pie' – you have one slice and have to come back for more! You'll find a recipe for vegan pastry on page 268, or you can buy some in the supermarket if you're short of time. Dice the veg small for best results – about 1.5–2cm.

**Filling**

2 tbsp olive oil

1 onion, finely chopped

2 large carrots, diced

200g celeriac, diced

100g sweet potato, pumpkin or
   squash, diced

3 leeks, cut into rounds

2 garlic cloves, finely chopped

100ml white wine

300ml vegetable stock

2 bay leaves

1 tbsp wholegrain mustard

a few sage leaves, finely chopped

a few sprigs of parsley,
   finely chopped

1 tbsp cornflour

100ml plant-based double cream

sea salt and black pepper

**Pastry**

250g vegan pastry
   (see p.268 or shop-bought)

flour, for dusting

**Glaze**

1 tbsp plant-based milk

1 tbsp olive oil

Heat the olive oil in a large sauté pan and add the onion, carrots and celeriac. Cook over a medium heat until they take on some colour, then add the sweet potato, pumpkin or squash, the leeks and the garlic. Continue to cook for a few minutes, then pour over the white wine. Bring to the boil and bubble until the wine has reduced by half.

Add the vegetable stock, season with plenty of salt and pepper and the bay leaves, then bring back to the boil. Turn the heat down, partially cover the pan and simmer until the vegetables are tender. Take the pan off the heat.

Remove the vegetables from the pan with a slotted spoon and put them on a pie dish or plate. Take out the bay leaves and discard. Simmer the remaining liquid until reduced by about a third, then whisk in the mustard and herbs.

Mix the cornflour with a little cold water until completely smooth, then whisk this into the liquid to thicken. Add the cream and stir to combine. Pour this over the vegetables and leave to cool. Preheat the oven to 200°C/Fan 180°C/Gas 6.

Roll the pastry out on a floured surface. Wet the edge of the pie dish or plate and carefully place the pastry over the filling. Trim and crimp. Mix the milk and oil together and brush over the pastry – this will help it brown nicely. Cut a couple of steam holes in the centre of the pie and decorate with offcuts if you like.

Bake for about 45 minutes until the pastry is a light golden brown and the filling is piping hot.

# Roasted aubergine pasta

SERVES 4

2 aubergines, cut into 2–3cm cubes
4 tbsp olive oil
1 onion, finely chopped
3 garlic cloves, finely chopped
100ml red wine
400g can of tomatoes
½ tsp chilli flakes
¼ tsp ground cinnamon
400g tube-shaped pasta
50g black olives, pitted and sliced
25g capers, rinsed
sea salt and black pepper

**To serve**
a few basil leaves, torn
a few shavings of hard vegetarian
sheep's cheese, such as Pecorino,
(optional)

A good gutsy pasta dish like this makes a perfect meal on a cold winter's night – or any time of year when you feel like something simple, tasty and comforting. We've roasted the aubergines in the oven instead of frying them, which takes so much oil, and we've added great flavour with spices, olives and capers. Tube-shaped pasta is best such as rigatoni, tortiglioni or ditali.

Preheat the oven to 200°C/Fan 180°C/Gas 6. Put the aubergine cubes on a couple of baking trays and drizzle up to 2 tablespoons of the oil over them. Sprinkle with salt and pepper, then roast for about 30 minutes, until tender and golden brown.

Meanwhile, heat the remaining oil in a large pan. Add the onion and cook gently until soft and translucent. Add the garlic and continue to cook for another 2 or 3 minutes. Turn up the heat, pour in the red wine and allow it to bubble up, then continue to cook until it has reduced down by half. Add the tomatoes and spices, season with salt and pepper, then cook for about half an hour until the sauce has thickened and reduced.

While the sauce is simmering, bring a large pan of water to the boil and add salt. Add the pasta and cook until tender but still with a little bite to it – al dente.

Add the olives and capers to the sauce, then stir in the roasted aubergines. Simmer for a few more minutes just to make sure everything is piping hot. Serve with the pasta, garnished with basil leaves and shavings of cheese, if using.

 *BIKER VEGAN TIP*

For a vegan dish, just leave out the cheese. Everything else is fine.

# Mediterranean-style vegetable bake

75ml olive oil

1 large onion, very finely chopped

½ red pepper, deseeded and very finely chopped

½ green pepper, deseeded and very finely chopped

2 garlic cloves, very finely chopped

1 tsp dried oregano

1 tsp dried thyme

½ tsp fennel seeds, lightly crushed

zest and juice of 1 lemon

400g salad potatoes, thinly sliced into rounds (or ovals)

2 large courgettes, thinly sliced into rounds

4 tomatoes, sliced into rounds (keep the juice)

16 black olives, pitted but left whole

sea salt and black pepper

**A dish full of sunshine! There are lots of baked vegetable dishes like this in Mediterranean cooking and they are just fantastic. Our version is simple to make, but just make sure you chop the onion and peppers up really fine so they collapse into a nice juicy purée. A perfect centrepiece for a veggie feast.**

First heat the oil in a frying pan. Add the onion and peppers and cook over a very gentle heat until the vegetables are soft and almost collapsed into a purée. This will take at least 20 minutes. Add the garlic, herbs, fennel seeds and lemon zest and season generously with salt and black pepper. Cook for a further couple of minutes, then remove the pan from the heat and set aside.

Cook the potato slices in plenty of boiling, salted water for 3–4 minutes until softened but still with a bit of bite to them. Drain and run the slices under a cold tap until they are cool enough to handle. Preheat the oven to 200°C/Fan 180°C/Gas 6.

Spread half the onion and pepper mix over the base of a large, shallow oven dish. Mix the potatoes, courgettes and tomatoes together and arrange them over the onion and peppers. Add any juice from slicing the tomatoes. Season with salt and pepper.

Pour over the rest of the onion and pepper mix and dot the olives around the dish. Mix the lemon juice with 2 tablespoons of water and pour this evenly over the vegetables.

Cover with foil and bake for 20 minutes, then remove the foil and bake for another 10–15 minutes until the vegetables are completely cooked through and slightly brown around the edges. Serve with a soft green salad and some crusty bread to mop up the delicious juices.

3 tbsp olive oil

2 fennel bulbs, each cut into
   8 wedges

4 turnips, each cut into 6 wedges

1 onion, finely chopped

2 garlic cloves, finely chopped

1 tsp ground ginger

1 tsp ground cumin

1 tsp ground coriander

1 tsp ground cinnamon

pinch of ground cumin

large pinch of saffron, soaked
   in warm water

500ml vegetable stock or water

1 ripe tomato, puréed

1 tsp maple syrup

50g green olives (pitted or unpitted)

1 preserved lemon, finely chopped

small bunch of parsley or coriander,
   chopped

sea salt and black pepper

**Chickpea garnish**

1 tbsp olive oil

150g chickpeas

1 tsp ras-el-hanout

**Couscous**

200g wholemeal couscous

1 tbsp olive oil

220ml tepid water

# Fennel & turnip tagine

**Both fennel and turnip caramelise well and their sweet flavours work beautifully with the olives and preserved lemon in this tasty tagine. When we first made this, we used honey for a touch of sweetness, but realised it's a great vegan recipe so changed to maple syrup. Ras-el-hanout is a spice mix, popular in North African cooking, and is available in supermarkets.**

Heat a tablespoon of the oil in a large flameproof casserole dish. Add the fennel bulb wedges and fry them over a medium-high heat until lightly caramelised on the cut edges. Remove and set aside, then caramelise the turnips in the same way. Remove and add the remaining olive oil.

Add the onion and cook gently over a lower heat until soft and translucent. Add the garlic and spices and stir for a couple of minutes, then put the fennel and turnip back in the pan. Stir until the vegetables are well coated, then pour in the saffron and its water and the stock. Stir in the tomato and the maple syrup.

Season with salt and pepper and bring to the boil. Turn down the heat and simmer for about 20 minutes until the vegetables are completely tender. Stir in the olives and preserved lemon.

To make the chickpea garnish, heat the oil in a frying pan and add the chickpeas. Sprinkle with the ras-el-hanout and season with salt and pepper. Fry, stirring regularly, until the chickpeas start to take on some colour.

For the couscous, put the couscous in a bowl and drizzle over the olive oil. Season with salt, then add the water and cover with a plate. Leave to stand until the water has been completely absorbed, then fluff up the couscous with a fork.

Garnish the tagine with the chickpeas and some chopped parsley or coriander and serve with the couscous.

# Chilli bean bake

2 tbsp olive oil

1 large onion, sliced into thin wedges

3 garlic cloves, finely chopped

200g squash or pumpkin, diced

½–1 tsp chilli flakes (to taste)

2 tsp dried sage or a few fresh sage leaves, shredded

100ml white wine or water

3 x 400g cans of cannellini beans (720–750g drained weight)

250g cherry tomatoes

200g sprouting or tenderstem broccoli, trimmed and roughly chopped

400g mozzarella, thickly torn or sliced

sea salt and black pepper

This is real comfort food and it's dead easy to put together. With a beautifully mellow flavour, creamy and spicy at the same time, it's just the thing for a cool autumn evening. It's great made with sprouting or tenderstem broccoli, but you can also use the lovely greens called cime di rapa (or less glamorously – turnip tops). They go really well with the sage, chilli and squash.

Heat the oil in a large sauté pan or a saucepan and add the onion. Cook gently over a medium heat until it starts to take on some colour, then add the garlic and the squash or pumpkin. Continue to cook for another 5 minutes, then sprinkle in some chilli flakes and the sage.

Season with salt and pepper and pour in the wine or water and the beans. Blitz 150g of the cherry tomatoes until smooth, then add these to the pan. Arrange the broccoli over the top, then bring the liquid to the boil. Turn the heat down to a simmer and cover until the broccoli has steamed to al dente.

Preheat the oven to 200°C/Fan 180°C/Gas 6.

Spoon the contents of the pan into a large ovenproof dish and cover with the mozzarella. Tuck the rest of the cherry tomatoes in between the mozzarella.

Bake in the preheated oven for about half an hour, or until bubbling and lightly browned. Serve sprinkled with a few more chilli flakes if you like. Nice with a crisp green salad.

200g okra

vinegar – white wine, red wine or cider

200g very ripe tomatoes

2 tbsp olive oil

200g sweetcorn kernels, preferably freshly shucked

1 onion, finely chopped

1 red pepper, deseeded and diced

200g small courgettes, cut into rounds

200g squash or pumpkin

3 garlic cloves, finely chopped

4 sprigs of tarragon, 2 left whole, 2 finely chopped

400g can of butter beans, drained

150g fresh or frozen broad beans (podded weight), remove the grey skins if you have time

sea salt and black pepper

# Succotash

A traditional dish in the USA, succotash is one of those things where everyone claims their version is the best. It does sometimes contain meat such as salt pork, but the key ingredients are beans and sweetcorn and often okra. We do recommend soaking the okra in vinegar, as below, because it takes away the sliminess which puts some people off this tasty vegetable. This is simple to make and very good to eat, so try it and see what you think. Best with freshly shucked corn when it's in season.

---

First prepare the okra. Trim the tops, then cut each piece into 3 or 4. Put them in a bowl and cover with vinegar, then leave to stand for half an hour, stirring occasionally. Rinse thoroughly and drain. Blitz the tomatoes to a purée in a blender or food processor and set aside.

Heat a tablespoon of the oil in a large flameproof casserole dish or a saucepan. Add the sweetcorn and toast until lightly browned. Remove from the pan and set aside.

Add the remaining oil and the onion and red pepper. Cook over a gentle heat until the onion is soft and translucent, then turn up the heat and add the courgettes, squash and okra. Continue to cook for a few minutes until the vegetables start to brown very slightly but are still firm.

Add the garlic and cook for a further 2 minutes, then put the sweetcorn back in the pan. Pour in the puréed tomatoes and add 500ml of water, then season with salt and pepper. Add the whole tarragon sprigs and stir in the butter beans and broad beans.

Bring to the boil, then turn down the heat and simmer until the vegetables are just tender. Stir in the remaining tarragon and serve piping hot.

Palak paneer & chickpeas 164

Stuffed crispy pancakes 166

Leek & goat's cheese tart 168

Stuffed cornbread 170

Black bean & chipotle tacos 172

Mushroom mini kievs 174

Aubergine katsu 176

Roast vegetable lasagne 178

Mushroom bourguignon cobbler 180

Caramelised onion, potato & greens galette 182

Vegetable biryani 184

Indian shepherd's pie 186

Mushroom risotto 188

Gnocchi with blue cheese sauce 190

Cauliflower tikka masala 192

Stuffed pasta shells 194

Biker burgers 196

Vegan pizzas 198

BBQ sauce & sausages 200

Dirty corn 200

Veggie enchiladas 202

Artichoke & fennel paella 204

Christmas veggie Wellington 206

# Palak paneer & chickpeas

**Palak paneer**

1 x 200–250g block of paneer, diced

1 tbsp lemon juice

1 tbsp coconut oil

½ tsp ground turmeric

1 tsp garam masala

1 onion, finely chopped

25g fresh root ginger, grated

3 garlic cloves, crushed or grated

200g spinach (frozen is fine)

small bunch of coriander

sea salt and black pepper

**Chickpeas**

1 tbsp coconut or olive oil

400g can of chickpeas, drained
   (or see p.270)

½ tsp Kashmiri chilli powder

1 tbsp lemon juice

**Yoghurt dressing**

2 tsp cumin seeds, lightly crushed

1 tbsp lemon juice

250g plain yoghurt

**To serve**

4 small naan breads, warmed
   through

aloo bhujia or similar

seeds from a pomegranate

coriander leaves

green chillies, finely sliced

In 2006, when filming in India, we both went palak paneer mad and it's a love affair that's lasted for years. Paneer is an Indian soft cheese, and in palak paneer it is cooked in a spicy spinach sauce. We serve it with naan bread, toasted chickpeas and other garnishes and it is mega good with lots of different flavours and textures. One of the garnishes is a crispy Indian snack called aloo bhujia – you've probably eaten this as part of a Bombay mix, but you can buy it on its own from Asian stores or supermarkets. All together this makes a great meal to share with friends. Just pile everything on the table and let everyone help themselves.

First make the palak paneer. Toss the paneer in the lemon juice and add half a teaspoon of salt. Heat the coconut oil in a frying pan and add the turmeric. Fry for a few seconds to combine, then add the paneer. Toss in the turmeric-coloured oil and fry on all sides until crisp.

Blitz the remaining ingredients for the palak paneer in a blender with 150ml of water and plenty of seasoning, then pour this round the paneer in the pan. Bring to the boil, then turn the heat down and simmer for several minutes until the sauce has reduced down a little and is piping hot.

For the chickpeas, heat the oil in a separate pan and add the chickpeas with some salt and pepper. Sprinkle in the chilli powder and lemon juice, and fry for a few minutes until there's a really aromatic smell from the toasting chickpeas.

For the yoghurt dressing, stir the cumin seeds and lemon juice into the yoghurt. If the mixture is very thick, thin it with a little water. Season with half a teaspoon of salt and some black pepper.

Arrange everything in bowls on the table. Everyone can pile some palak paneer on to warm naan bread, then top with chickpeas, aloo bhujia and yoghurt dressing. Garnish with pomegranate seeds, coriander leaves and chillies and spoon more of the palak paneer sauce over the top if you like.

# Stuffed crispy pancakes

**Cheese sauce**

500ml whole milk

slice of onion

a few cloves

2 bay leaves

a few peppercorns

2 blades of mace

50g butter

65g plain flour

100g mature vegetarian Cheddar, grated

sea salt and black pepper

**Spinach**

450g spinach

generous rasping of nutmeg

**Pancakes**

125g plain flour

2 eggs

300ml whole milk

oil, for frying and brushing

**To assemble**

50g plain flour

100g dry breadcrumbs

2 eggs

We used to love frozen crispy pancakes when we were kids – remember them? We've done our own meat version in the past, and now here's a veggie recipe to delight your taste buds.

For the sauce, put the milk in a pan with the onion and spices and bring to the boil. Take the pan off the heat and leave to infuse until tepid. Melt the butter in a separate pan, then add the flour and stir for several minutes until the rawness of the flour is cooked out. Strain the milk and gradually add it to the roux, whisking thoroughly with each addition to make a thick, smooth sauce. Season, then stir in the cheese until it has melted. Set aside to cool.

Wash the spinach well, then push it down into a pan over the heat until it has wilted. Chop it with scissors while still in the pan, then press it through a sieve until it is as dry as it can be – you should have about 200g. Season well with salt, pepper and nutmeg.

For the pancakes, put the flour in a bowl and add a pinch of salt. Beat in the eggs, then gradually whisk in the milk to make a thin batter. Rub a small pancake pan (about 18cm in diameter) with oil, add a ladleful of batter and swirl it around. Cook until the batter has set on the underside, then flip the pancake and cook on the other side. Remove and repeat until you've used all the batter (there should be enough for 8 pancakes), then leave to cool.

Preheat the oven to 200°C/Fan 180°C/Gas 6 and line 2 baking trays with lightly oiled baking paper. Put the flour on one plate, the breadcrumbs on another and beat the eggs in a bowl.

Divide the sauce and spinach between the pancakes (use about 75g of the sauce and 25g of the spinach per pancake). Brush round the edges of each with beaten egg and seal tightly, making sure there are no air pockets. Dip each pancake in the flour, pat off the excess, then dip in the egg and lastly the breadcrumbs.

Arrange the pancakes on the baking trays and brush each one with a little oil. Bake for 20 minutes until they are crisp and golden brown and the filling is liquid and piping hot.

# Leek & goat's cheese tart

1 portion of shortcrust pastry
(see p.268) or 500g block
of shop-bought

flour, for dusting

**Filling**

1 tbsp olive oil

25g butter

4 or 5 leeks (about 400g trimmed
weight), finely sliced into ½ cm
rounds

a few sprigs of thyme

2 garlic cloves, finely chopped

50ml white wine, vermouth or water

4 eggs, well beaten

300ml double cream

1 tbsp Dijon mustard

200g vegetarian goat's cheese
(2 x 100g rounds with rind), sliced

grating of nutmeg

sea salt and black pepper

There's nothing like a good tart, and leeks and goat's cheese
are a marriage made in heaven. We used the log-shaped goat's
cheese with a rind and you don't have to remove the rind so
there's no waste. Place the end slices with the rind facing down
and it will soften into the egg and cream mixture.

Roll out the pastry on a lightly floured work surface and use it
to line a 28cm round tart dish. Prick the pastry base all over with
a fork, then chill for at least half an hour. Preheat the oven to
200°C/Fan 180°C/Gas 6.

Line the pastry with baking paper, fill with baking beans and cook
in the oven for 10 minutes. Remove the beans and paper and put
the dish back in the oven for another 5 minutes until the pastry
is set but has not taken on much colour. Leave to cool. Lower the
oven temperature to 180°C/Fan 160°C/Gas 4.

Put the oil and butter in a large lidded sauté pan. When the butter
starts foaming, add the leeks, a couple of sprigs of thyme and the
garlic, then season. Stir until the leeks are glossy with butter, then
cook gently for several minutes over a low heat. Add the liquid,
cover and leave to braise for at least 10 minutes, or until the leeks
are tender. Remove from the heat and leave to cool.

Mix the eggs and cream together in a bowl and season with salt
and pepper. Do not whisk as you don't want the mixture to be
aerated, but make sure everything is well combined.

Spread the mustard over the pastry, then top with the leeks. Pour
in the eggs and cream mixture, then arrange the slices of cheese
over the top. Add a couple more sprigs of thyme and finely grate
over some nutmeg.

Bake for 35–40 minutes until the topping has just set and is lightly
browned – some wobble in the centre is a good thing but make
sure it isn't liquid. Serve hot or at room temperature. Fermented
tomatoes (see p.260) would be nice on the side.

## Filling

1 red pepper, deseeded and sliced

2 red onions, cut into thin wedges

200g butternut squash or pumpkin, diced

2 tbsp olive oil

6 garlic cloves, left unpeeled

1 tsp dried thyme or rosemary

200g vegetarian Cheddar or other hard cheese, grated

50g pickled jalapeños

sea salt and black pepper

## Cornbread batter

150g fine cornmeal

½ tsp bicarbonate of soda

400g can of creamed sweetcorn or 400g sweetcorn, puréed

240ml buttermilk

2 eggs, beaten

50g butter or vegetable oil

# Stuffed cornbread

This was inspired by a dish cooked by Julia Vinson, one of the mums in our *Mums Know Best* telly series. It's a smashing supper dish, perhaps with some green veg or a salad on the side and it also goes well with the succotash on page 158. It's a great addition to a picnic feast too. This isn't a typical cornbread, as the layers are quite thin and it doesn't have that slightly sandy texture that some cornbreads have.

First make the filling. Preheat your oven to 200°C/Fan 180°C/Gas 6. Put the pepper, onions and squash or pumpkin in a roasting tin. Season with salt and pepper and drizzle with the oil. Roast for 20 minutes, then add the garlic cloves and sprinkle over the dried thyme or rosemary. Roast for a further 15–20 minutes until the vegetables are tender and slightly charred. Squish out the garlic flesh from the skins and set aside.

Make the cornbread batter. Mix the cornmeal, bicarbonate of soda and half a teaspoon of salt in a bowl. Beat in the sweetcorn, buttermilk and eggs to make a wet, pourable mixture.

Heat the butter or oil in an ovenproof skillet or a flameproof casserole dish with a base diameter of about 23cm. Measure out half of the batter – it's best to do this with a measuring jug rather than by eye as it's easy to overestimate – and pour it on to the hot butter or oil. Arrange the vegetables over the batter, then top with the cheese and the jalapeños. Pour over the remaining batter. Don't worry if the filling pokes through the batter.

Bake for about 45 minutes until the top is a rich brown and firm to the touch. Serve hot, with green vegetables or salad.

**Guacamole**

juice of 1 lime

2 avocados, peeled

1 small garlic clove, finely chopped

1 medium tomato, finely chopped

¼ red onion, finely chopped

a few sprigs of coriander,
    finely chopped

sea salt and black pepper

**Chipotle sauce**

chipotle paste

1 portion of vegan cream sauce
    (see p.262) or 200g plant-based
    coconut yoghurt

**Black beans**

1 tbsp olive oil

1 onion, finely chopped

3 garlic cloves, finely chopped

1 tsp ground oregano

1 tsp ground cumin

¼ tsp ground cinnamon

¼ tsp ground allspice

250g black beans
    (from a can or see p.274)

**Broccoli**

250g sprouting or tenderstem
    broccoli

1 bunch of spring onions, trimmed

2 tbsp olive oil

**To serve**

12–16 corn tortillas

lime wedges

coriander leaves

# Black bean & chipotle tacos

**Everyone loves this sort of meal where you can dig in and help yourself to a bit of this and a bit of that. It's all really good stuff and, although there are a fair number of ingredients, nothing is tricky to make. Look for the corn tortillas rather than the flour and corn mix, as they work better for this dish.**

First the guacamole. Put the lime juice in a bowl with a good half teaspoon of sea salt. Mash in the avocados and add the garlic, tomato, onion and coriander. Stir and set aside. To make the chipotle sauce, add the chipotle paste to the cashew cream or yoghurt. Start with a teaspoon, then taste and increase until it is as hot as you like it.

For the beans, heat the oil in a pan and add the onion. Cook gently until soft and translucent, then add the garlic, oregano and spices. Cook for another couple of minutes, then add the beans and about 50ml of water. Season, stir to combine, then heat gently. Set aside to keep warm. Preheat the oven to 180°C/Fan 160°C/Gas 4.

Wash the broccoli and shake off any excess water but don't dry it completely. Arrange the broccoli and spring onions on a baking tray and drizzle over the oil. Season, then roast in the oven until the vegetables are lightly charred and tender. Check after 10 minutes – they should be done but may take longer. Roughly chop the spring onions and place on a serving dish with the broccoli.

Meanwhile, warm the tortillas. Line a bowl or basket with a tea towel and heat a dry frying pan (preferably not a non-stick one). Heat each tortilla in the pan until very lightly browned but still soft and pliable – this should take about 20 seconds on each side. Put them in the basket and cover with the tea towel to keep warm. Make up the tacos or pile everything on the table with some lime wedges and coriander leaves and let people help themselves.

## Garlic butter

75g butter, softened

3 fat garlic cloves, crushed

leaves from a few sprigs of tarragon, finely chopped

leaves from a few sprigs of parsley, finely chopped

1 tsp lemon zest

## Mushroom mixture

25g butter

1 onion, very finely chopped

2 garlic cloves, very finely chopped

250g mushrooms, very finely chopped

1 tbsp porcini powder or 15g dried mushrooms, blitzed to a powder

1 tsp dried thyme

600g floury potatoes, unpeeled and cut into chunks

sea salt and black pepper

## To finish

50g plain flour

2 eggs

100g breadcrumbs – dried, fine crumbed sort, not panko

vegetable oil, for deep-frying

# Mushroom mini kievs

The wonderful thing about a chicken kiev is that centre of melting garlicky butter that oozes out voluptuously when you cut into it. We thought there's no reason for vegetarians to be denied that pleasure, so we came up with this brilliant idea, as mushrooms and garlic butter are a classic combo. These are not difficult to make but you do have to be very careful not to overcook them. Too long in the deep-fryer or the oven and the butter will start steaming and might burst out, so watch the timing carefully. These go down a real treat with a glass of beer.

First make the garlic butter. Mash everything together, then form the mixture into 8 quenelles (egg shapes) of about 10g each. Use 2 dessert spoons to shape them, then put them on a plate and open-freeze them until completely solid.

To make the mushroom mixture, heat the butter in a frying pan and add the onion. Cook gently over a medium heat until lightly caramelised, then add the garlic and mushrooms. Cook until the mushrooms have reduced, and the mixture is very dry. Stir in the porcini powder or blitzed dried mushrooms and the thyme.

Put the potatoes in a steamer basket and steam over boiling water for about 20 minutes. Drain, remove the skins and then mash, preferably with a potato ricer. This method makes a nice dry mash. Mix with the mushroom mixture and season, then chill.

Divide the mushroom and potato mixture into 8 portions. Remove the butter from the freezer and shape a portion of the mixture around each piece of butter – making oval shapes similar to scotch eggs or chicken kievs. Chill for at least half an hour until firm.

Put the flour, one of the eggs and half the breadcrumbs on individual plates. Dip each kiev in the flour, pat off the excess, coat in the egg and then roll in the breadcrumbs. Then dip each one in the egg and the breadcrumbs for a second time and put them on a baking tray. When you have used up the first lot of egg and breadcrumbs, add the rest to the plates and continue until all the kievs are coated. Chill again for about half an hour.

To cook, half-fill a deep saucepan or a deep-fat fryer with oil and heat to about 180°C. Do not leave the pan unattended.

Fry the kievs a couple at a time for a few minutes until golden brown. Keep an eye on them the whole time and as soon as you are happy with the colour remove – the longer you leave the kievs in the oil, the more danger there is of them bursting. Drain them on kitchen paper and serve immediately while hot.

Alternatively, you can bake them. Preheat the oven to 200°C/Fan 180°C/Gas 6. Brush the kievs with oil, then bake for 10–15 minutes, checking regularly after 10. The longer the kievs cook, the greater the risk that they might burst.

SERVES 4

# Aubergine katsu

We've used lovely meaty aubergine slices for our veggie version of this Japanese favourite. And we prefer to bake the aubergines rather than fry them, as they seem to soak up gallons of oil that way – but if you want to deep-fry, just go ahead. One word sums this up – tasty. A belter of a dish.

**Katsu sauce**

2 tbsp vegetable or coconut oil

1 onion, finely chopped

100g sweet potato, finely diced

3 garlic cloves, finely chopped

10g fresh root ginger, grated

2 tbsp medium curry powder

1 tbsp plain flour

400ml vegetable stock

1 tbsp mango chutney

1 tbsp tomato ketchup

1 tbsp soy sauce

1 tbsp maple syrup

½ tsp sesame oil

sea salt and black pepper

**Pickles**

6 radishes, thinly sliced

½ cucumber, cut into long ribbons

1 tsp salt

1 tsp caster sugar

3 tbsp rice wine vinegar

**Breaded aubergines**

2 large aubergines,
    cut into 1cm rounds

100g plain flour

panko breadcrumbs

vegetable oil, for brushing

**To serve**

1 tsp black sesame seeds

4 spring onions, cut in half
    lengthways and shredded
    as finely as possible

First make the sauce. Heat the oil in a saucepan and add the onion and sweet potato. Fry over a medium heat until the vegetables take on some colour around the edges. Add the garlic, ginger, curry powder and flour and continue to cook for another 2–3 minutes, stirring until everything is well combined.

Add the stock along with the chutney, ketchup, soy sauce and maple syrup. Season with salt and pepper. Bring to the boil, then turn the heat down and simmer, stirring regularly, until the vegetables are cooked through. Add the sesame oil and blitz everything in a food processor until smooth. Taste and add more seasoning, ketchup or maple syrup if you need to. Set aside.

Next make the pickles. Put the vegetables in a bowl and sprinkle with the salt, sugar and vinegar. Transfer to a colander and leave to drain for half an hour.

For the aubergines, preheat the oven to 200°C/Fan 180°C/Gas 6. Mix the flour with about 150ml of water until you have a smooth batter the thickness of double cream – if it seems too thick, add a little more water. Season with salt. Immerse the aubergine slices in the batter, then one by one, remove, shake off any excess and dip in the breadcrumbs. Make sure all the sides are well covered.

Brush 2 baking trays generously with oil, then arrange the aubergine slices on them. Brush the slices with more oil. Bake for 30–35 minutes, turning once, until the aubergines are cooked through and the breadcrumbs are golden.

Drizzle the sauce over the aubergines and serve with the pickles. Garnish with sesame seeds and spring onions.

# Roast vegetable lasagne

**Roast vegetables**

3 red onions, cut into thin wedges

3 peppers (2 red, 1 green), deseeded and cut into strips lengthways

250g squash or pumpkin, peeled and cut into thin slices

500g courgettes, cut into thin rounds

1 garlic bulb, separated into unpeeled cloves

2 tsp mixed dried Italian herbs

2 tbsp olive oil

sea salt and black pepper

**Béchamel sauce**

800ml whole milk

1 slice of onion

4 cloves

2 bay leaves

2 blades of mace

60g butter

60g flour

**To assemble**

½ portion of tomato sauce, quite liquid (see p.263)

12 lasagne sheets

basil leaves

250g block of vegetarian mozzarella, torn into pieces

50g vegetarian Parmesan-style cheese, grated

A great dish for a weekend feast, lasagne can be put together earlier in the day, ready to pop in the oven when you want.

---

Preheat the oven to 200°C/Fan 180°C/Gas 6. Arrange the vegetables and garlic on 2 roasting trays and season. Sprinkle with the herbs and drizzle with olive oil. Roast for 40–45 minutes, turning the veg over a couple of times, until everything is tender and lightly browned in places. Leave to cool. Squeeze the garlic flesh from the skins, mash it up and mix it into the vegetables.

To make the béchamel, heat the milk with the onion, cloves, bay leaves and mace to boiling point. Remove it from the heat, leave to cool and then strain. Melt the butter in a clean pan and add the flour. Stir to combine then cook and stir for several minutes. Add the milk, a ladleful at a time, and stir until completely combined before adding more. You should have a pourable sauce.

Take a rectangular ovenproof dish, about 30 x 20cm or a bit bigger, and spread a small ladleful of tomato sauce over the base, then a large ladleful of the béchamel. Place 3 lasagne sheets on top, followed by another small ladleful of the tomato sauce, a third of the vegetables and a few torn basil leaves. Season, then ladle over more béchamel and top with another 3 sheets of lasagne.

Repeat these layers twice so you have 3 layers of vegetables, then pour the remaining béchamel over the last sheets of lasagne. If you have any tomato sauce left over, put spoonfuls of it on top of the béchamel. Arrange the mozzarella over the top and sprinkle over the grated cheese.

Bake in the oven for about 30 minutes until the top is brown and bubbling. Leave the lasagne to stand for at least 10 minutes before serving, so it will be easier to cut into portions.

 **BIKER VEGAN TIP**

For a vegan dish, make the béchamel with olive oil and plant-based milk, then top the lasagne with a breadcrumb and herb mix instead of cheese. Delicious.

SERVES 4

# Mushroom bourguignon cobbler

**This is a really special dish with a rich, almost meaty, flavour. It's one of the recipes we couldn't quite decide on – should we make it a pie, a crumble or a cobbler? So we asked you on Instagram and you voted by a slim margin for a cobbler topping. We've used blue cheese in ours but if you're not a fan, a veggie Cheddar would be fine too.**

2 tbsp olive oil

12 button onions or shallots, peeled and left whole

300g carrots, cut into chunks

½ tsp sugar

25g butter

750g mushrooms (mix of portobello, chestnut, button, cremini), thickly sliced

1 large sprig of thyme

2 bay leaves

a few sage leaves, finely chopped

200ml red wine

300ml mushroom or vegetable stock

1 tbsp mushroom ketchup

1 tsp Dijon mustard

parsley, finely chopped, to serve

sea salt and black pepper

**Cobbler topping**

200g self-raising flour

1 tsp baking powder

½ tsp salt

1 tsp dried sage

50g vegetarian blue cheese, crumbled

1 egg, beaten

75ml buttermilk

First make the bourguignon. Heat the oil in a large flameproof casserole dish and add the onions or shallots and the carrots. Fry over a high heat, stirring regularly, until they are dappled with dark brown patches. Sprinkle over the sugar and continue to cook for another couple of minutes to help caramelise. Remove them from the dish and set aside.

Add the butter to the casserole dish. When it starts to foam, add the mushrooms and cook over a high heat until they have reduced down. Put the onions and carrots back in the dish and season generously with salt and pepper. Add the herbs, then pour in the red wine. Bring to the boil and leave to bubble until the wine has reduced by at least a third. Add the stock, mushroom ketchup and mustard and stir until completely combined.

Bring back to the boil, then turn down to a simmer and cover with a lid. Cook for half an hour, perhaps a little longer, until the vegetables are completely tender. Preheat the oven to 200°C/Fan 180°C/Gas 6.

Meanwhile, make the cobbler topping. Put the flour and baking powder into a bowl and add half a teaspoon of salt. Add the sage and the cheese, then mix in the egg and buttermilk to make a fairly sticky dough. Form the dough into 12 small balls and space them out over the top of the bourguignon. Cover and simmer for 10 minutes, then transfer the dish to the oven, uncovered, for a further 10–15 minutes until the cobbler topping has puffed up and is lightly browned. Serve in shallow bowls with a garnish of finely chopped parsley.

SERVES 4

2 tbsp olive oil

4 medium red onions,
    cut into thin wedges

3 garlic cloves, finely chopped

1 tbsp sherry vinegar

leaves from a large sprig of thyme,
    plus more for garnish

300g kale or chard

1 tsp lemon zest

1 portion of shortcrust pastry
    (see p.268) or 500g block of
    shop-bought

flour, for dusting

250g new or salad potatoes,
    cooked and sliced

125g vegetarian Cheddar or other
    hard cheese, grated

1 egg, beaten

sea salt and black pepper

# Caramelised onion, potato & greens galette

**This dish made it to the cover of our book – enough said! Galette is a nice French word for a rustic-looking tart. Instead of being baked in a tin with neatly crimped edges, a galette is more free-form and made on a baking tray, with the pastry being folded over some of the filling. If it looks a bit rough and ready that's all part of the charm, so relax and enjoy.**

Heat the oil in a frying pan. Add the onions and cook over a fairly high heat until they have softened to al dente and started to caramelise. Add the garlic and continue to cook for a couple of minutes. Season with plenty of salt and pepper, drizzle over the sherry vinegar, then add the thyme leaves and stir. Cook for another minute, then remove the pan from the heat, tip everything into a bowl and set aside to cool.

Next prepare the greens. If the leaves are large, pull them from their stems. Keep any smaller leaves whole. Wash the leaves well, then without shaking off any excess water, add them to the frying pan and cook until they have wilted down. Stir through the lemon zest and season with salt and pepper. Set aside.

Preheat the oven to 200°C/Fan 180°C/Gas 6. Lightly flour a work surface and roll out the pastry into a round with a diameter of about 35cm. Transfer to a large baking tray (don't worry if the pastry overlaps it a bit at this stage).

Arrange the onions over the pastry, leaving a border of about 4–5cm around the edge. Toss the potatoes, greens and cheese together and arrange them on top of the onions. Sprinkle with more thyme. Fold in the pastry border so it partially covers the filling – you will find that most of the filling is left exposed.

Brush the pastry with the beaten egg. Bake in the oven for about 40 minutes until the pastry is golden brown. Serve hot or cold.

**Fried onions**

vegetable oil

2 large onions (about 300g),
  thinly sliced into crescents

1 tsp cumin seeds

sea salt and black pepper

**Rice**

300g basmati rice

juice of ½ lemon

**Vegetables and sauce**

250g carrots

300g cauliflower

300g runner beans, de-stringed

1 tbsp vegetable oil

5 cardamom pods

1 x 5cm piece of cinnamon stick

1 star anise

3 cloves

2 bay leaves

4 fat garlic cloves, crushed

15g fresh root ginger, grated

½ tsp mild chilli powder

1 tsp ground cumin

½ tsp ground turmeric

1 tsp garam masala

3 tbsp coriander stems,
  finely chopped

1 large tomato, diced

150ml plain yoghurt

juice of 1 lime

**Toppings**

1 large pinch of saffron

30g butter

50ml single cream

**Garnish**

sliced green chillies

sprigs of coriander

lime wedges

# Vegetable biryani

**A biryani is a celebration dish – a feast for a special occasion. There are lots of elements, but nothing is difficult. Just make sure you don't overcook the cauliflower, don't stint on rinsing and soaking the rice and don't overcook it. Stick to these rules and you'll be fine.**

First start the onions. Cover a large frying pan with a thick layer of vegetable oil and fry the onions over a medium to high heat until they are crisp and dark brown. Keep stirring regularly to make sure they don't burn. Add the cumin seeds for the last few minutes, then season generously with salt and pepper. Drain the onions on kitchen paper and set aside.

Put the rice in a large bowl and cover with water. Swill a couple of times until the water is cloudy, then drain. Repeat until the water is fairly clear. Leave the rice to soak for 30–45 minutes.

While the rice is soaking, prepare the vegetables. Slice the carrots and runner beans on the diagonal and cut the cauliflower into small florets. Bring a large pan of water to the boil and add plenty of salt. Add the carrots and simmer for 5 minutes, then add the cauliflower and beans. Continue to cook for another 3–4 minutes until the carrots are just tender but still firm and the cauliflower is al dente. It's very important that the cauliflower shouldn't be cooked through, so check after 3 minutes.

Heat the oil in a large flameproof casserole dish. Add the whole spices and bay leaves and fry for a minute, then add the garlic, ginger and remaining spices. Stir for a couple of minutes, then stir in the rest of the ingredients. Season and add the vegetables. Remove the dish from the heat and set aside.

For the topping, toast the saffron in a dry frying pan, then leave it to cool. Put it in a mortar with a pinch of salt and grind it to a fine powder with the pestle. Add 2 tablespoons of just-boiled water and leave to stand. Preheat the oven to 200°C/Fan 180°C/Gas 6.

When the rice has been soaked, bring a large pan of water to the boil and add 2 teaspoons of salt and the lemon juice. Add the rice and cook for 4–5 minutes until it is almost but not quite cooked through. When you squeeze a grain of rice it should break up into several pieces and still be firm, not mushy. Drain, but don't shake dry – it needs some residual moisture. Taste the rice and add more salt if you like.

Add a third of the fried onions to the vegetables and sauce in the casserole dish and stir. Add another third to the rice, then spoon the rice over the vegetables. Melt the butter and add the cream, then pour this over the rice. Finally, drizzle over the saffron water.

Cover the dish with 2 layers of foil. Put it over a high heat, then as soon as you can hear the contents bubble and the foil starts to puff up a little from the steam, put the dish in the oven for about 20 minutes.

Remove the dish from the oven and leave to stand for 15 minutes before removing the foil. The rice should be beautifully dry and fluffy. Add the last of the onions.

Serve with the green chillies, coriander, lime wedges and some raita (see p.262)

# Indian shepherd's pie

**Everyone loves this one. It's a good old shepherd's pie but with a filling of veg curry and a topping of spicy mash – which is great on its own, too. If you're vegan, use plant-based milk and leave out the butter and cheese and it's still great. Do cut the veg nice and small – half centimetre dice or smaller is perfect.**

1 tbsp oil

1 large onion, very finely chopped

1 large carrot, coarsely grated

1 celery stick, very finely diced

1 green or red pepper, deseeded and very finely diced

100g celeriac, turnip or swede, very finely diced

100g butternut squash, very finely diced

200g green beans, sliced into rounds

25g fresh root ginger, finely chopped

2 garlic cloves, finely chopped

1 tbsp mild curry powder

500ml vegetable stock or water

100g cooked brown lentils

1 tsp tamarind paste

2 tsp Pickapeppa sauce or mushroom ketchup

1 tbsp cornflour or arrowroot

sea salt and black pepper

**Masala potato topping**

1kg floury potatoes (Maris Pipers or King Edwards are good), unpeeled and cut into chunks

2 tbsp groundnut or vegetable oil

1 tsp cumin seeds

1 tsp mustard seeds

1 onion, finely chopped

1 green chilli, finely chopped

100ml plant-based or regular milk

25g butter (optional)

small bunch of coriander, chopped

100g vegetarian Cheddar, grated (optional)

olive oil or butter

Heat the oil in a large pan and add all the vegetables. Cook them over a medium-high heat, stirring regularly, until they start to brown and soften, then add the ginger, garlic and curry powder. Cook for another 2–3 minutes, stirring constantly, until well combined, then season.

Pour in the stock or water, and add the lentils, tamarind paste and Pickapeppa sauce or mushroom ketchup. Bring to the boil, then partially cover the pan and turn down the heat. Simmer for up to 30 minutes, until the vegetables are completely tender. Mix the cornflour or arrowroot with cold water to make a smooth, runny paste, then stir this into the vegetables. Simmer, stirring constantly, until the sauce thickens.

For the topping, bring a large pan of water to the boil, add the potatoes and season with salt. Simmer for 10–15 minutes until the potatoes are knife tender, then drain well and tip them back into the pan. Leave over a low heat to steam off excess water.

Heat the oil in a frying pan and add the cumin and mustard seeds. When the seeds start popping, add the onion and chilli. Cook over a medium-high heat until the onion has browned.

Mash the potatoes with the milk and add the butter, if using. Add the onion mixture and chopped coriander and mix thoroughly. Preheat the oven to 200°C/Fan 180°C/Gas 6.

Put the filling in a large, 30 x 20cm, ovenproof dish. Spread the potato evenly on top, then sprinkle over the cheese, if using. Rough up the surface with a fork and drizzle over a little oil or add knobs of butter. Bake the pie for 25–30 minutes until nicely browned and piping hot.

# Mushroom risotto

25g dried wild mushrooms

2 tbsp olive oil

50g butter

1 large onion, finely chopped

500g mushrooms, 200g finely chopped, 300g sliced

3 garlic cloves, finely chopped

300g risotto rice

100ml white wine

a few sprigs of thyme

about 1.25 litres mushroom stock, warmed through

squeeze of lemon juice

50g vegetarian Parmesan-style cheese, grated, plus extra to serve

handful of parsley, very finely chopped

a few drops of truffle oil (optional)

sea salt and black pepper

**Wild mushrooms do make an extra-special risotto, but they do cost an arm and a leg, so we usually use a good mixture of button, field and chestnut mushrooms. Then we add some lovely extra flavour with a few soaked dried mushrooms. Mushroom stock really helps too – you can buy some in stock pots or cubes, or see our recipe on page 277 if you want to make your own.**

Soak the dried mushrooms in a small bowl of warm water for half an hour or so. Heat a tablespoon of the olive oil with 25g of the butter in a large sauté pan. Add the onion and cook gently until it's soft and translucent.

Strain the dried mushrooms and rinse them to get rid of any grit. Reserve the soaking liquid after straining off the sediment. Finely chop the soaked mushrooms and put them in the pan with the onion, then add the 200g of finely chopped fresh mushrooms. Cook over a medium-high heat until the mushrooms have given off their liquid and it has evaporated. Add the garlic and cook for another couple of minutes.

Pour in the risotto rice and stir until it is glossy. Pour in the wine and leave to bubble until most of it has evaporated. Add the soaking liquid and thyme to the stock. Season the rice, then turn down the heat and start adding the hot stock a ladleful at a time, stirring constantly in between each addition. Make sure most of the liquid has been absorbed before you add more. When the rice is al dente and creamy, stop adding stock – you may not need it all. Add a squeeze of lemon juice and stir.

Add the remaining butter and the cheese and beat them into the risotto for extra creaminess. Remove the pan from the heat and cover it with a lid while you prepare the mushroom garnish.

Heat the remaining oil in a frying pan and add the 300g of sliced fresh mushrooms. Fry over a high heat until golden brown, then season. Serve the risotto in bowls, garnished with the fried mushrooms, chopped parsley, a drizzle of truffle oil, if using, and extra cheese grated or shaved over the top.

## Gnocchi

425g floury potatoes (Maris Pipers or King Edwards are good), unpeeled and cut into chunks

400g can of chickpeas, drained and skinned or cook your own (see p.270)

100g '00' pasta flour, plus extra for dusting

1 egg

olive oil

salt

## Blue cheese sauce

1 tbsp olive oil

25g butter

1 onion, finely chopped

2 garlic cloves, finely chopped

12 large sage leaves, finely shredded

125g vegetarian blue cheese, crumbled

## To serve

30g walnuts, toasted and finely chopped

# Gnocchi with blue cheese sauce

Dave cooked gnocchi for our French producer and the blue cheese sauce was his idea. Pretty good, eh? Made with a mix of chickpeas, potato and flour, these are brilliant and not that difficult. Just be gentle with the dough and don't bash it about too much. It's fine to make these in advance and reheat them in the sauce when you're ready to eat. Amazing.

---

First make the gnocchi. Put the potatoes in a steamer basket and steam over boiling water for about 20 minutes until perfectly tender. While they are steaming, roughly purée the chickpeas in a food processor, then mash until smooth – the best way to do this is with a potato ricer. They should feel floury to touch. Put the flour in a mound on a clean work surface and add the mashed chickpeas. Season with plenty of salt.

When the potatoes have finished cooking, put them in a dry saucepan and cover with a tea towel. Leave to steam over a low heat for a few minutes to make sure they are completely dry. Peel while the potatoes are still hot – the skins should come away easily. If you have a potato ricer, mash the still-hot potatoes directly on to the flour and chickpeas. Alternatively, mash the potatoes in the pan and add immediately.

Make a well in the centre of the flour, chickpea and potato mound and add the egg. Work everything together as gently as you can to make a smooth dough. Clean your work surface and flour it well, then pat the dough out into a 20cm square. Cut the square into strips of 1.5cm wide, then roll each strip into a cylinder. Cut each cylinder into 1.5cm lengths and dust with more flour.

You can leave the gnocchi like this, or you can shape them with a fork or a gnocchi paddle. Use a very light touch as they are quite fragile. Put each one on the paddle, press down lightly to make an indentation and pull very slightly towards you at the same time – you will find you have groove marks on the outer side which will curl in around the indentation. To use a fork, simply mark with the prongs on one side and indent on the other.

Bring a large saucepan of salted water to the boil. You'll need to cook the gnocchi in several batches, so you don't overcrowd the pan. They are done when they float to the top, which should take between 30 seconds and a minute. Remove with a slotted spoon and toss each batch with a small amount of olive oil. Reserve the cooking water.

To make the sauce, heat the oil and butter in a large sauté pan. Add the onion and cook over a medium heat until the onion is soft and lightly coloured. Add the garlic and cook for another couple of minutes.

Add the sage leaves and the blue cheese and stir until the cheese has melted. Add a few spoonfuls of the gnocchi cooking water and whisk.

Add the gnocchi to the pan and gently fold them into the sauce so they are all coated, thinning the sauce with a little more cooking water if necessary.

Serve sprinkled with a tablespoon of the finely chopped walnuts.

1 large cauliflower, broken into florets

400g can of chickpeas, drained (optional)

**Marinade**

150ml Greek yoghurt

1 tbsp olive oil

juice of 1 lemon

1 tsp Kashmiri chilli powder

1 tsp garam masala

½ tsp nigella seeds

sea salt and black pepper

**Sauce**

1 onion, finely chopped

3 garlic cloves, finely chopped

15g fresh root ginger, chopped

1 tbsp coconut or olive oil

1 tsp Kashmiri chilli powder

1 tsp ground cumin

1 tsp ground coriander

1 tsp garam masala

½ tsp ground cinnamon

¼ tsp ground cloves

800ml passata or 2 x 400g cans of tomatoes puréed until smooth

50g butter (optional)

50ml double cream

pinch of sugar (optional)

**To serve**

coriander leaves

lemon wedges

naan bread or basmati rice

# Cauliflower tikka masala

In Pakistan apparently, they call cauliflower (gobi) 'vegetarian meat' – we've no idea why. Maybe because it looks like a giant brain! Cauliflower tikka is all the rage, so we've taken it one step further to make it into a lovely rich tikka masala. You can add chickpeas too, if you like, for a bit of extra protein. Superb.

---

Preheat the oven to 200°C/Fan 180°C/Gas 6. Mix all the marinade ingredients together and season with salt and pepper. Add the cauliflower florets and turn them over in the marinade until completely coated. Place them, well spaced out, on a baking tray and roast for 20–25 minutes, turning them over halfway through, until lightly browned and tender to the point of a knife.

To make the sauce, purée the onion, garlic and ginger together in a food processor until smooth. Heat the oil in a large saucepan and add the purée. Fry for a few minutes, stirring regularly, until it thickens, then sprinkle in all the spices and fry for another couple of minutes.

Pour in the passata or puréed tomatoes and season with salt and pepper. Bring to the boil, then turn the heat down and simmer for a few minutes until the sauce has reduced by about a third.

Add the butter, if using, and whisk to make sure it combines with the sauce. Stir in the cream, then taste. If the sauce tastes acidic, add a pinch of sugar. Add the cauliflower and the chickpeas, if using, and cook for a few minutes to make sure everything is piping hot but don't let it boil. Garnish with plenty of coriander and lemon wedges and serve with naan bread or basmati rice.

 **BIKER VEGAN TIP**

For a vegan version, use plant-based yoghurt in the marinade. Then for the sauce, use vegan cream sauce (see p.262) instead of the butter, and plant-based yoghurt instead of cream. This gives a lighter, sweeter result.

SERVES 4

200g large pasta shells
1 portion of tomato sauce
   (see p.263)
vegetable oil, for brushing

**Stuffing**
3 tbsp olive oil
1 onion, finely chopped
1 small courgette, grated
2 garlic cloves, finely chopped
a few sprigs of rosemary,
   finely chopped
75g almonds, very finely chopped
25g breadcrumbs
zest and juice of 1 lemon
300g spinach, wilted down
   (frozen is fine)
handful of basil leaves, shredded
sea salt and black pepper

**Topping**
1 tbsp olive oil
1 garlic clove, cut in half
50g breadcrumbs
25g almonds, very finely chopped
a few basil leaves, very finely
   shredded

# Stuffed pasta shells

This is vegan without even trying. We both usually like loads of grated cheese on a pasta bake, but with this tasty almond topping you really don't need it. A proper good filling supper this, and one that we're sure you're going to love. Look out for the big pasta shells which will be labelled conchiglioni. The little ones – conchiglie – are too small to stuff.

For the stuffing, heat 2 tablespoons of the oil in a frying pan, add the onion and cook gently until soft and translucent. Add the courgette and continue to cook until it has wilted down, then add the garlic and rosemary and cook for a further 2 minutes. Remove from the heat, tip the mixture into a bowl and leave to cool.

Heat the remaining oil in a pan and add the almonds and breadcrumbs. Toast for a few minutes over a low to medium heat until very lightly toasted. Remove from the heat and leave to cool. Mix with the onion and courgette mixture, then add the lemon zest and juice, the spinach and basil. Season and mix thoroughly.

Cook the pasta in plenty of salted water, until just al dente, then drain and rinse under cold water until cool enough to handle.

Make the topping. Heat the oil in a frying pan and add the garlic. Fry for a minute or so, just to flavour the oil, making sure the garlic doesn't take on any colour. Remove the garlic from the pan and discard, then add the breadcrumbs and almonds. Stir to combine and cook until very lightly toasted as before. Season and remove the pan from the heat, then add the basil leaves and set aside. Preheat the oven to 200°C/Fan 180°C /Gas 6.

Lightly brush a large oven dish with oil. Fill each shell with a heaped teaspoon of the stuffing – just enough so the shells will still close comfortably – and place them in the oven dish. Pour the tomato sauce over the pasta, then sprinkle the breadcrumb mix on top. Bake for about 30 minutes until the topping is crisp and brown and the pasta is piping hot.

# Biker burgers

1 small onion (about 75g), very finely chopped, almost to a purée

400g can of black beans, drained and very lightly broken up or mashed, or cook your own (see p.274),

50g cooked brown rice

2 tbsp tomato ketchup

1 tsp mushroom ketchup

1 tsp soy sauce

½ tsp garlic powder

¼ tsp liquid smoke (optional) OR use smoked salt

75g dried breadcrumbs

1 egg

sea salt and black pepper

**Burger sauce**

1 tbsp tomato ketchup

2 tbsp mayonnaise

½ tsp Dijon mustard

1 tsp pickle juice (from the gherkin jar)

½ tsp onion powder

**To serve**

vegetable oil, for frying

4 slices of vegetarian cheese (optional)

4 burger buns

slices of red onion

slices of tomato

4 large gherkins, sliced or left whole to go on the side

4 leaves of soft lettuce

Veggie and vegan burgers have come such a long way and now it's time to throw our latest version into the mix. It's quite a simple recipe – and the better for it we think – and great with the burger sauce. If you don't want to do the whole bun thing, how about going the French route and serving the burgers with salad and chips? Can't go wrong.

Put all the burger ingredients in a bowl and season well with regular or smoked salt and black pepper. Mix thoroughly – the mixture will feel very wet but knead it together for a few moments and you will feel it start to firm up. Divide the mixture into 4 equal-sized patties and put them in the fridge or freezer to chill. Leave in the fridge for at least an hour or chill in the freezer for 15 minutes.

Make the burger sauce. Mix all the ingredients together and season with salt and pepper, then taste and adjust as necessary. Put the sauce in the fridge until you need it.

Heat a tablespoon of vegetable oil in a non-stick frying pan and fry the burgers until well browned on both sides. If you want to make cheeseburgers, add a slice of cheese to each burger when you have flipped them for the first time. Cover the pan with a lid (or an upturned wok) until the cheese has started to melt.

Wipe the frying pan clean and lightly toast the burger buns, cut-side down. This will help stop them from becoming soggy. Build the burgers with as many of the garnishes as you like and serve immediately.

 **BIKER VEGAN TIP**

For a vegan burger, leave the egg out of the mixture and don't add any cheese. Use vegan mayo in the sauce.

## Pizza dough

500g strong white flour,
   plus extra for dusting

2 tsp instant yeast

1½ tsp salt

2 tbsp olive oil

300ml tepid water

## Tomato sauce

100g tomato purée (from a jar, tin
   or tube – not passata)

2 tomatoes, roughly chopped

50g pitted olives – any colour

1 garlic clove, grated

handful of basil leaves

1 tbsp olive oil

generous pinch of chilli flakes
   (optional)

pinch of sugar

sea salt and black pepper

## Topping

4 medium salad potatoes, very thinly
   sliced (1–2mm)

2 small or 1 large courgette, very
   thinly sliced (about 1mm) or
   4–6 artichoke hearts, sliced

1 tbsp olive oil

a few rasps of lemon zest

a few sprigs of rosemary,
   finely chopped

2 tbsp capers

## To finish

4 large handfuls of rocket

2 tbsp olive oil

1 tsp balsamic vinegar

# Vegan pizzas

**We're normally pizza purists, but these beauties really fit the bill. We wanted to make a pizza that didn't need cheese and we've got so many great flavours here you really don't miss it at all. Pizzas are easy to make, but we find the tricky bit is transferring them to the oven, so assembling them on a piece of baking paper helps a lot. You'll be a pizza chef in no time.**

First make the pizza dough. Put the flour into a bowl with the yeast. Mix thoroughly and add the salt. Add the oil and work in the water. Mix to form a dough, then leave it to rest for half an hour. Turn out on to a floured work surface and knead for about 10 minutes until soft and elastic. Put the dough back into a bowl and cover with a damp tea towel. Leave it to stand until doubled in size – this will take at least an hour.

Preheat the oven to its highest temperature and put 2 baking trays into the oven to heat – 4 if you have them.

Put all the tomato sauce ingredients into a food processor and blend until broken down and almost, but not quite, smooth. Taste and season.

Bring a pan of water to the boil and season with salt. Add the potatoes and cook for 3 minutes, then drain. Mix with the courgette or artichokes, oil, zest and rosemary and season with more salt and pepper.

Divide the dough into 4 even pieces and roll each piece out as thin as you can make it – if you can see through it in patches, that's good. Each base should be about 30cm in diameter. Transfer each base to a piece of baking paper to assemble.

Spread a quarter of the sauce over each base, then arrange the potatoes, courgette or artichokes and the capers over the top. Bake for 7–10 minutes until speckled with brown and cooked through. Remove and leave to stand for a few minutes. Mix the rocket with the olive oil and balsamic vinegar and pile on top of the pizzas. Serve immediately.

# BBQ sauce & sausages

**The sausages are great as they are but even better with the barbecue sauce. If you're not vegan, you can use butter instead of oil for the sauce.**

---

**Sauce**

1 tbsp vegetable oil

1 small onion, finely chopped

3 garlic cloves, finely chopped

¼ tsp allspice

¼ tsp cloves

¼ tsp cumin

30ml cider vinegar

50ml apple juice

50ml maple syrup

25g dark soft brown sugar

100ml tomato ketchup

50g tomato purée or paste

1 tbsp soy sauce

1 tbsp mushroom ketchup

1–2 tsp chipotle paste or similar smoky chilli sauce (or to taste)

sea salt and black pepper

**Sausages
(see pp.98–99)**

Heat the oil in a small pan and add the onion. Fry, stirring frequently, until the onion is cooked through and has caramelised around the edges. Add the chopped garlic and cook for another 2 or 3 minutes. Stir in the spices.

Add the cider vinegar and apple juice. Bring to the boil and simmer until reduced by half. Stir in all the remaining ingredients and add 100ml of water. Season with salt and pepper. Bring back to the boil, then turn the heat down and simmer very gently for half an hour. The sauce will reduce and thicken and the flavours will blend together. Taste and add more seasoning or chilli, if you like. For a smooth sauce, blend and push it through a sieve.

Gently fry the sausages, brushing them with the sauce for the last couple of minutes. Serve the sauce with the sausages and store any leftovers in a jar in the fridge.

# Dirty corn

4 large heads of corn with husks on, or 4 cobs, wrapped in foil

100g vegetarian goat's cheese or feta, crumbled

small bunch of coriander, finely chopped

4 spring onions, finely chopped

2 tsp smoked chilli powder or flakes

zest of 2 limes

4 tbsp mayonnaise

wedges of lime, to serve

**We've reworked this recipe from one we wrote for our *Route 66* TV series last year and it's better than ever. Basically the corn is cooked in its husks, or wrapped in foil, on the barbecue and then slathered with mayo and cheese – what more could you want? A crumbly goat's cheese works well or you can use a vegetarian feta if you can find it.**

---

Get the barbecue going. While the coals are heating, prepare the corn. Trim off the tassles and remove the outer layer of husk, then put the heads of corn on to the barbecue rack and cover. Grill for 5 minutes, then uncover and continue to cook for another 10–15 minutes, turning regularly. You can tell how evenly you

have turned the corn if there are deep char marks all the way round. During this time the cobs will steam in their husks or foil wrappings and any remaining husks will char.

Check for doneness – the kernels should have changed to a bright yellow and started to char in places. Remove the husks or foil and put the cobs back on the barbecue for another minute or so, turning frequently, to char some more.

Crumble up the cheese and mix with the coriander, spring onions, chilli powder or flakes and the lime zest. Divide the mixture between 4 plates. Slather each cob with mayonnaise, then dip them into the cheese mixture. Serve with wedges of lime.

### Sauce

3 green peppers, deseeded and cut in half

6 jalapeños or mild green chillies, left whole

6 garlic cloves, unpeeled

bunch of spring onions, trimmed

2 tbsp olive oil

100g tomatillos or green tomatoes or 100g cucumber, diced

zest and juice of 1 lime

bunch of coriander

sea salt and black pepper

### Filling

1 tbsp olive oil

2 red onions, finely chopped

1 red pepper, deseeded and finely diced

2 garlic cloves, finely chopped

400g can of pinto beans or red kidney beans, drained

1 tsp dried oregano

1 tsp ground cumin

½ tsp ground cinnamon

½ tsp ground allspice

### To assemble

8 corn tortillas

200g soured cream

150g vegetarian Cheddar, grated

### To serve

any leftover soured cream

lime wedges

coriander leaves

# Veggie enchiladas

If you grow your own tomatoes and end up with some green ones in the autumn this is a great way to use them. Tomatillos are lovely here too, if you can find any. Otherwise, the cucumber is good and adds a hit of savoury to the pepper sauce. As for the chillies, jalapeños are nice for this and quite mild, but if you prefer to blow your socks off, try adding a bird's-eye chilli. Look for corn tortillas rather than flour ones, as they are more robust and won't go soggy.

---

Preheat the oven to 220°C/Fan 200°C/Gas 7. Place the peppers, jalapeños or chillies, garlic and spring onions on a large baking tray and drizzle them with oil. If using tomatillos or green tomatoes, add them too, but if using cucumber leave it until later – it doesn't need cooking. Roast for 20 minutes, then start checking for doneness. The vegetables will cook at different rates – you want them collapsing down a little and charring. When all the vegetables are charred in places, remove them from the oven.

Reduce the oven temperature to 200°C/Fan 180°C/Gas 6. Put the green peppers in a bowl and cover it with a plate. Leave to steam until cool enough to handle, then remove the skins. Remove the seeds from the chillies and squish the flesh out of the garlic. Roughly chop the spring onions.

Put all the roasted vegetables into a food processor with the remaining sauce ingredients (including the cucumber, if using) and plenty of seasoning. Pulse until you have a coarse, fairly liquid sauce. Set aside.

To make the filling, heat the olive oil in a sauté pan and add the onions and red pepper. Cook gently over a medium heat until the onions are soft and starting to take on some colour. Add the remaining filling ingredients along with 50ml of water and plenty of seasoning. Simmer until piping hot, then gently mash the beans so some of them break down. Remove from the heat.

To assemble, put a small ladleful of the green sauce in the base of an ovenproof dish. Lightly toast each tortilla in a dry frying pan, then add a tablespoon of the filling. Top with a teaspoon of soured cream, then roll up and place in the dish.

Repeat with all the tortillas, making sure they don't quite touch, then pour over the remaining green sauce. Sprinkle over the cheese, then bake in the oven for about 30 minutes until the tortillas have browned round the edges and the cheese is bubbling.

Serve with any remaining soured cream, lime wedges and some fresh coriander.

# Artichoke & fennel paella

4 tbsp olive oil

2 fennel bulbs, trimmed and cut into wedges

1 large onion, finely chopped

1 green pepper, deseeded and diced (optional)

3 garlic cloves, finely chopped

a few sprigs of thyme

a few sprigs of rosemary

2 tsp sweet paprika

1 litre vegetable stock

1 large pinch of saffron

1 tbsp tomato purée

2 strips of pared lemon zest

250g paella rice

400g can of cannellini beans, drained

150g green beans

6 chargrilled artichoke hearts, halved (from a jar or deli counter)

sea salt and black pepper

**To serve**

chopped parsley

lemon wedges

We've done paella recipes before but always with meat or fish, so we fancied having a crack at a veggie version. In fact, this one is vegan with no trouble at all and is really tasty. Be sure to get proper paella rice as it absorbs the stock beautifully – regular short-grain just doesn't cut it. You'll find chargrilled artichoke hearts in jars at the supermarket or at the deli counter  and they are delicious.

Heat 2 tablespoons of the oil in a paella pan or a large sauté pan. Add the fennel wedges and fry them over a high heat, turning them regularly, until caramelised on all the cut sides. Remove from the pan and set aside.

Add the remaining oil to the pan and gently cook the onion and green pepper over a medium heat until very soft and starting to caramelise. Add the garlic, thyme and rosemary, then sprinkle in the paprika and stir for another couple of minutes.

While the onion and pepper are cooking, heat the stock in a saucepan to boiling point, then add the saffron, tomato purée and lemon zest. Season with salt and pepper, remove from the heat and leave the stock to infuse until you are ready to use it.

Add the rice to the pan and stir for a minute or so to coat it with the flavoured oil. Spread it over the pan as evenly as you can, then pour in the stock. Arrange the beans, fennel, green beans and artichoke hearts over the rice.

Bring to the boil, then turn down the heat and cook – trying to avoid stirring – until the rice is still on the firm side of al dente and most of the stock has been absorbed. This should take about 20 minutes over a gentle heat. Remove the pan from the heat, cover with foil, and leave to stand for 10 minutes.

Serve garnished with chopped parsley and lemon wedges.

# Christmas veggie Wellington

**Both our families have vegetarians and vegans at the Christmas dinner table, and this used to be a challenge. The Hairy Biker nut roast has been our staple for years but now it's time for a change. We've taken it to the next level and hope this great feast pleases you and your family as much as it does ours.**

## Filling

1 tbsp olive oil

25g butter

1 onion, finely chopped

1 celery stick, finely chopped

200g root vegetables, coarsely grated

2 garlic cloves, finely chopped

leaves from a sprig of thyme, finely chopped

a few sage leaves, finely shredded

zest of 1 lemon

¼ tsp ground allspice

¼ tsp ground cloves

¼ tsp ground mace

100g cooked chestnuts, roughly chopped

50g nuts, finely chopped

75g cooked wild or brown rice

75g cooked brown lentils

25g breadcrumbs

2 tsp mushroom ketchup

1 tsp soy sauce

1 egg, beaten

sea salt and black pepper

## Mushroom duxelles

1 tbsp olive oil

25g butter

2 shallots, very finely chopped

400g mushrooms, very finely chopped into 3mm dice (use a food processor if you like)

2 garlic cloves, finely chopped

200g spinach

squeeze of lemon juice

First make the filling. Heat the oil and butter in a large frying pan and add the onion and celery. Cook until the onion is starting to caramelise, then add the grated root vegetables. Continue to cook, stirring regularly, until they have reduced down considerably. Season with salt and pepper and stir in the garlic and herbs. Continue to cook for another 2–3 minutes then stir in the lemon zest and spices. Set aside to cool. When cool, stir in all the remaining ingredients and set aside.

To make the mushroom duxelles, heat the oil and butter in a frying pan and add the shallots. Cook gently until translucent, then add the mushrooms and garlic. Cook until the mushrooms have reduced down in volume and any liquid has evaporated away – the texture should almost be that of a mushroom pâté. Wilt down the spinach in a little water, then drain and finely chop. Squeeze out as much water out as you can, then stir the spinach into the mushrooms and add the lemon juice.

Put the prunes in a small saucepan and cover with the sherry. Bring to the boil, then remove from the heat and leave the prunes to absorb the sherry. Preheat the oven to 200°C/Fan 180°C/Gas 6. Line a baking tray with baking paper.

To assemble, dust a large piece of baking paper with flour and place it on your work surface. Roll out the puff pastry to a rectangle measuring about 30 x 40cm. Spread a quarter of the mushroom mixture lengthways down the middle of the puff pastry, leaving a border on both short sides. Pile half the filling mixture on top, then put a line of the prunes along the centre. Add the rest of the filling, making sure it seamlessly joins together, then spread the rest of the mushroom mixture over the top and sides of the filling.

Brush the edges of the pastry with beaten egg, then bring up the sides to cover the filling and slightly overlap it. Seal the ends, then carefully roll the Wellington on to the baking tray so the join is on the bottom. Cut a few slashes in the top and brush with more egg. Bake for about 35 minutes or until it is a rich golden brown and piping hot. Leave to stand for 10 minutes before slicing. Serve with the cranberry sauce and gravy. Roast potatoes and parsnips (see p.250) and sautéed greens (see p.257) complete the festive spread.

**Prunes**

12 prunes

75ml oloroso sherry

**Pastry**

flour, for dusting

500g block of puff pastry

1 egg, beaten, for sealing
   and brushing

# Cranberry sauce

Put the cranberries, orange or clementine zest and juice and the sugar into a pan. Add a splash of water and cook over a gentle heat, stirring to dissolve the sugar. When most of the cranberries have burst and the sauce has thickened, taste and add a little more sugar if necessary. Stir in the oloroso or port and simmer for another minute. Transfer to a serving bowl and allow to cool.

**Cranberry sauce**

250g fresh or frozen cranberries

grated zest and juice of 1 orange
   or 2 clementines

50g caster sugar

1 tbsp oloroso sherry or port

# Gravy

Heat the olive oil and butter in a saucepan. Add the shallot and fry over a medium-high heat until softened and caramelised. Add the mushrooms and cook until they have reduced down and are dry. Stir in the garlic and thyme and season with salt and pepper.

Stir in the flour and cook for a couple of minutes, stirring constantly, then turn up the heat and add the wine or sherry. Bring to the boil, stirring constantly, then add the mushroom ketchup and stock a little at a time until you have a fairly thin gravy. Check the seasoning and strain if you like.

**Gravy**

1 tbsp olive oil

25g butter

1 shallot, finely chopped

200g mushrooms, very finely
   chopped

1 garlic clove, finely chopped

a sprig of thyme, leaves finely
   chopped

1 tbsp plain flour

100ml white wine or dry sherry

1 tbsp mushroom ketchup

250ml mushroom stock
   (see p.277 or shop-bought)

 **BIKER VEGAN TIP**

Leave out the egg from the filling, replace any butter with more oil and use vegan puff pastry. Mix a tablespoon of plant-based milk with a tablespoon of olive oil to seal and brush the pastry.

Puddings & bakes

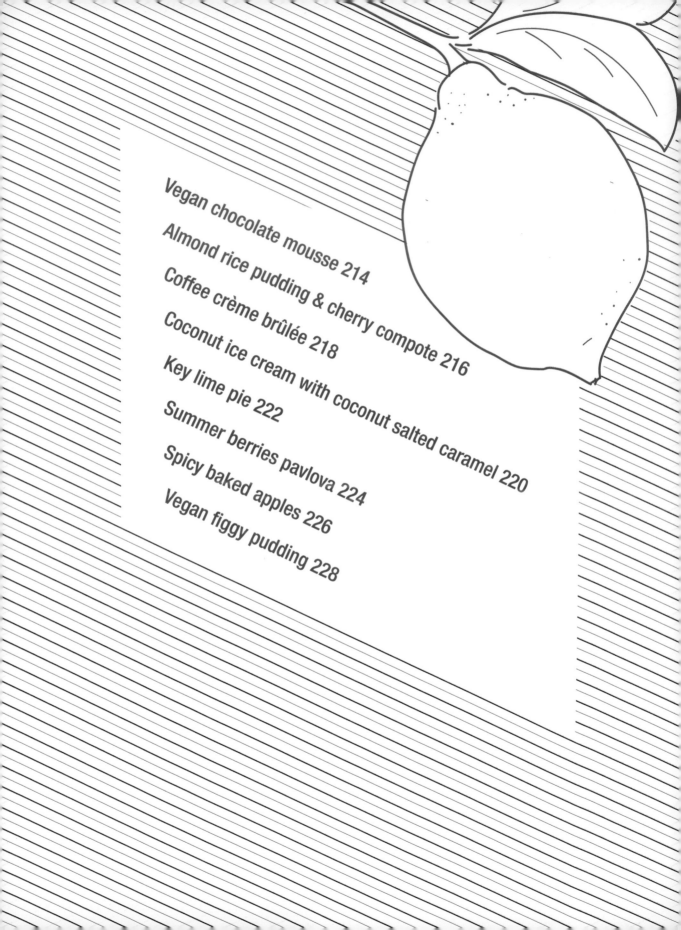

Vegan chocolate mousse 214

Almond rice pudding & cherry compote 216

Coffee crème brûlée 218

Coconut ice cream with coconut salted caramel 220

Key lime pie 222

Summer berries pavlova 224

Spicy baked apples 226

Vegan figgy pudding 228

Apricot clafoutis 230

Jammy dodgers 232

Orange polenta cake 234

Lemon bundt cake 236

Banana tray bake 238

Oatmeal chocolate chip cookies 240

Dairy-free brownies 242

Vegan Christmas cake 244

150ml aquafaba (liquid from a can of unsalted chickpeas)

30g caster sugar

175g vegan dark chocolate, broken up

50ml coconut milk (from a carton, not a can)

1 tsp vanilla extract

pinch of salt

25ml rum or spiced rum

**To serve (optional)**

a few coffee beans or squares of vegan chocolate

# Vegan chocolate mousse

Something magic happens to the water (called aquafaba) in a can of chickpeas when you whisk it for long enough. It turns into something that looks just like whisked egg whites and can be used in the same way to make awesome vegan versions of treats such as chocolate mousse. Just check the can of chickpeas to make sure they are unsalted. This mousse is light, airy, 100 per cent delicious – and just a little bit naughty with the dash of rum. Try it and see for yourselves.

First whisk the aquafaba. You'll need an electric hand-held whisk or a stand mixer, as this will take up to 15 minutes and that's a lot of elbow grease! Start whisking and, after the first minute or so, start adding the sugar, a teaspoon at a time. Continue to whisk until the aquafaba has reached the stiff peak stage, then set aside.

While the aquafaba is whisking, melt the chocolate. Break up the chocolate and put it in a heatproof bowl. Place the bowl over a pan of simmering water (don't let the bottom of the bowl touch the water) and stir the chocolate regularly so it melts evenly. Remove from the heat and leave to cool for a few minutes.

Whisk the coconut milk and vanilla extract into the chocolate, along with the salt. The mixture may go a little grainy but don't worry, just add the rum and beat vigorously and it will become smooth and glossy again. Leave to cool.

When the chocolate mixture is at room temperature, start incorporating the whisked aquafaba. Using a metal spoon, add a couple of large spoonfuls and fold them in carefully, trying to keep as much of the volume of the aquafaba as possible. Add the rest of the aquafaba and continue to mix until it is fully combined.

Divide the mixture between glasses or ramekins and leave to set in the fridge. Don't worry if the mousse appears quite liquid at this stage – it will firm up in the fridge. Serve with a small amount of coffee bean or chocolate grated over the top if you like.

# Almond rice pudding & cherry compote

200g short-grain rice (you can use paella or risotto rice)

up to 1.2 litres almond milk

50g caster sugar

75g flaked almonds

a few drops of almond extract (optional)

sea salt

**Cherry compote**

300g pitted black cherries (frozen are fine)

50g caster sugar

2 tsp cornflour

1–2 tbsp kirsch or cherry liqueur (optional)

squeeze of lemon juice

Almond milk makes a cracking vegan rice pud and you can add flaked almonds and almond extract if you like for extra flavour. We like to serve this with a beautiful cherry compote and don't worry – you can use those frozen pitted cherries from the supermarket if you don't fancy taking the stones out of fresh ones. This is good hot or cold, so you can take some to work for a snack, or if you have any compote left over it's great with the American pancakes on page 30 for breakfast.

First make the rice pudding. Put the rice in a large saucepan with a litre of the milk, the sugar, almonds and the almond extract, if using. Add a generous pinch of salt.

Slowly bring the milk to the boil, stirring every so often, then turn down the heat to a steady simmer. Continue to cook until the rice has absorbed most of the milk and is no longer translucent. This will take up to half an hour and when it is ready you should be able to drag a clear path across the base of the pan with your wooden spoon. It's fine to make the rice pudding in advance up to this point if you like.

For the compote, put the cherries, sugar and 100ml of water into a pan and simmer until the sugar has dissolved. Mix the cornflour with a little water until you have a smooth paste, then stir this into the cherries. Keep stirring until the mixture thickens, then add the kirsch or cherry liqueur, if using, and the lemon juice.

If not serving the pudding immediately, you may need the additional reserved milk to reheat it. To reheat, add the milk and stir until the pudding has loosened up but is still creamy.

Serve the rice pudding hot or well chilled with the cherry compote spooned over the top.

SERVES 4

**Prunes**
125g soft prunes, finely chopped
2 tbsp dark soft brown sugar
75ml Armagnac, brandy or similar

**Crème brûlée**
100g unsalted cashew nuts,
   soaked overnight
100ml strong coffee
400ml almond milk
80g caster sugar
2 tbsp cornflour
1 tsp vanilla extract
pinch of salt

**Topping**
4 tbsp granulated sugar

# Coffee crème brûlée

We've taken one of the most dairy-laden of all desserts and made it vegan. It still tastes fabulously decadent but it's a bit kinder to your waistline. It's made extra luxurious by the addition of booze-soaked prunes in each dish. A genius recipe that's mouth-wateringly good to eat.

First the prunes. Put them in a saucepan with the sugar and Armagnac or brandy. Simmer gently, stirring until the sugar has dissolved, then remove from the heat and leave to cool or until most of the liquid has been absorbed by the prunes. Divide the prunes between 4 large ramekins. If there is any liquid left, add it to the ramekins with the prunes.

To make the crème brûlée mixture, put the cashew nuts in a saucepan of water and bring to the boil. Boil for 5 minutes. Drain and put the cashews in a blender with the coffee. Blitz until the mixture is completely smooth.

Put all but a ladleful of the milk into a saucepan and add the sugar. Mix the cornflour with the reserved ladle of milk until you have a smooth, thin paste. Gently heat the milk, stirring until the sugar has dissolved, then whisk in the cornflour mixture. Add the vanilla extract and salt, then stir until the mixture has formed a thick but pourable custard. Add to the blender and blitz with the coffee and cashew nut purée.

If the mixture is at all grainy, push it through a fine sieve, then divide it between the 4 ramekins. Leave to cool, then transfer them to the fridge until very well chilled and set.

Before serving, sprinkle each ramekin with a tablespoon of sugar and either put them under a hot grill or use a blow torch over the top until the sugar has caramelised and set to a hard, crisp layer.

# Coconut ice cream with coconut salted caramel

**Salted caramel is so on-trend, darlings, and it's extra good with coconut. This ice cream is rich and delicious and you can make it without an ice cream machine. A simply fab dessert – totally vegan and totally good.**

### Ice cream

2 x 400ml cans of coconut milk

175g caster sugar

a few drops of coconut extract (optional)

30g cornflour

sea salt

### Salted caramel sauce

400ml can of coconut milk

75g light soft brown sugar

### Toasted coconut

50g desiccated or flaked coconut

First start the ice cream. Put 725ml of the coconut milk into a saucepan. Add the sugar, a generous pinch of salt and the coconut extract, if using. Stir over a low heat to dissolve the sugar.

Whisk the remaining coconut milk with the cornflour, making sure there are no lumps. Add this to the pan and stir over a low heat until the mixture thickens to a thick, pourable custard. Leave to cool completely, then chill for several hours.

To make the caramel, put the coconut milk into a saucepan with the sugar and a large pinch of salt. Stir over a low to medium heat until the mixture reduces by about half and will coat the back of a spoon. The colour should be a light caramel. Leave to cool, then tip into a bowl and chill.

For the coconut, toast it in a frying pan until lightly coloured and aromatic. Add a pinch of salt and leave to cool. Whizz briefly in a food processor to form crumbs.

Pour the mixture into a shallow container to a depth of about 4cm. Freeze for an hour or until the mixture has frozen around the edges. Then with an electric hand-held whisk, whisk until the mixture is uniformly combined. Repeat at least another 2 or 3 times until the ice cream is too firm to whisk. Leave to set completely. If you do have an ice cream machine, churn the chilled mixture until thick and transfer it to the freezer to set.

To serve, remove the ice cream from the freezer and leave in the fridge for half an hour before serving. Serve drizzled with the sauce and sprinkled with the toasted coconut.

**Crust**
200g vegan ginger biscuits,
75g non-dairy spread

**Filling**
300g block of silken tofu, drained
100ml lime juice
zest of 2 limes
125g caster sugar
50g coconut oil
3 tbsp cornflour
pinch of sea salt

**To serve**
250ml plant-based double cream
2 tbsp icing sugar, sieved
lime zest

# Key lime pie

It's been a challenge to take the dairy out of some our favourite desserts but with a bit of clever thinking, we found it's perfectly possible. Our vegan version of this classic American treat will amaze and delight you. Quick and easy to make, it's a great one when you're entertaining, as you can make the pie the day before and top it with cream just before serving.

---

Line a 20cm loose-bottomed tin or flan case with baking paper.

Crush the biscuits to fine crumbs, either in a food processor or by putting them into a bag and bashing them with a rolling pin. Gently melt the non-dairy spread in a pan, then stir in the biscuit crumbs. Mix thoroughly, press into your prepared tin, then leave in the fridge to chill for half an hour. Preheat the oven to 160°C/Fan 140°C/Gas 3.

To make the filling, blitz everything together until smooth. Pour this over the chilled crust.

Place the tin on a baking tray and bake in the preheated oven for 45–55 minutes until just set – it should still have a slight wobble in the middle. Try not to touch the top, though, as you will leave fingerprints. Just shake it gently to test.

Remove from the oven and leave to cool to room temperature before chilling for several hours, preferably overnight. Carefully remove from the tin before serving.

To serve, whip the cream to form soft peaks and fold in the icing sugar and lime zest. Swirl this mixture over the lime filling.

SERVES 6

**Meringue**
250–300ml aquafaba (liquid from
2 cans of unsalted chickpeas)

175g caster sugar

½ tsp cream of tartar

pinch of salt

1 tsp white wine vinegar

1 tsp vanilla extract

**Cream**
300ml plant-based cream

2 tbsp icing sugar

**Fruit**
750g berries – strawberries,
raspberries, redcurrants,
blackberries, blueberries

# Summer berries pavlova

When we were planning this pavlova, we couldn't decide whether to top it with passion fruit or berries, so we asked you guys. Our Instagram poll came back pretty close but the berries just edged it, so that's what we've done here. Aquafaba is the incredible liquid in a can of chickpeas that acts like egg white to make a meringue. Reducing it before whisking helps make the meringue more stable, but do this well in advance, so the aquafaba has time to chill completely.

Pour the aquafaba into a pan and place over a medium-high heat until reduced to 120ml. Leave to cool and then chill.

Preheat the oven to 150°C/Fan 130°C/Gas 2. Trace a 23cm circle on a piece of baking paper and place it on a baking tray.

Put the aquafaba in the bowl of a stand mixer. Whisk at high speed until it reaches soft peak stage – this will take at least 5 minutes, perhaps longer. Mix the sugar with the cream of tartar and a pinch of salt and start adding this a tablespoon at a time while the motor is still running until it is all incorporated and you have very glossy stiff peaks. Keep whisking while you add the vinegar and vanilla extract. If you don't have a stand mixer, use an electric hand-held whisk, but it will take some time.

Pile the meringue on to the baking paper and spread it into a round within the circle, leaving a border of about 2cm to allow for spreading. Make the sides slightly higher than the centre and create peaks by lightly touching the meringue with your spatula and pulling away quickly.

Put the meringue in the oven and immediately reduce the temperature to 120°C/Fan 100°C/Gas ½. Leave to cook for at least 2–2½ hours until the meringue is firm and very lightly browned. Turn the oven off, open the door very slightly and leave the meringue until it has cooled completely.

Just before you are ready to serve, whisk the cream with the icing sugar until it is thick enough to pile into the centre of the pavlova. Top with the fruit and tuck in.

75g softened butter, plus extra for greasing

1 tbsp maple syrup

2 tbsp light soft brown sugar

pinch of salt

1 tsp ground cinnamon

½ tsp mixed spice

1 tsp ground ginger

1 tbsp whisky, bourbon or calvados (optional)

1 tbsp lemon juice

75g raisins

2 balls of stem ginger, finely chopped

40g pecans or walnuts, finely chopped

6 large eating apples

**Whisky cream (optional)**

125ml thick double cream

2 tbsp whisky, bourbon or calvados

1 tbsp light soft brown sugar

1 tbsp syrup from stem ginger jar (optional)

# Spicy baked apples

A forgotten classic. Our mams always used Bramleys for baked apples, but you don't see them so much now and we find that large eating apples work just as well – and they don't burst like Bramleys often do. The whisky cream is a real treat but if you don't fancy it, serve the apples with double cream or ice cream. The ginger adds great flavour and you'll find jars of stem ginger in syrup in the supermarket.

Preheat the oven to 170°C/Fan 150°C/Gas 3½. Take an oven dish in which the apples will fit quite snugly and grease it with butter.

Mix the butter, maple syrup and sugar together with a generous pinch of salt and the spices. Gradually work in the whisky and lemon juice to make a smooth paste, then mix in the raisins, stem ginger and pecans or walnuts. Set aside.

To prepare the apples, make sure they all sit straight and trim the bases of any that are very lopsided. Using an apple corer or a paring knife, cut a 2–3cm hole in the top of the apple around the stem. Core the apple to about three quarters of the way down, making sure you take out all the seeds. Prepare all the apples in the same way. Press the filling mixture into the cavities, piling it into a dome on top.

Bake for 35–45 minutes, depending on the size of your apples. Start checking after about 25 minutes to make sure the dried fruit isn't burning. If it is getting too dark, place a piece of foil on top, but don't seal the dish with it. Remove the apples from the oven as soon as they are tender to the point of a knife.

To make the cream, if using, lightly whisk the double cream until it is thick and no longer pourable. Mix together the alcohol, sugar and stem ginger syrup, if using, to dissolve the sugar, then stir this into the cream. Whisk again to make sure it is holding its shape.

Serve the apples with any buttery juices from the dish spooned over the top and the cream, if using.

150g soft dried figs, quite finely chopped

100ml marsala wine or strong tea

100g plain flour

1 tsp baking powder

1 tsp mixed spice

50g breadcrumbs

pinch of salt

50g non-dairy spread, plus extra for greasing

75g dark soft brown sugar

150g carrot, finely grated

50ml aquafaba (liquid from a can of unsalted chickpeas), lightly whisked

# Vegan figgy pudding

Being Bikers, we couldn't have a book without a good old-fashioned steamed pud, like our mothers used to make. Those were the days. And here is a vegan version that you can serve with some vegan custard (see page 264). As you will see, we use aquafaba, that amazing water in a can of chickpeas, instead of an egg to bind the mixture.

Put the figs in a saucepan and add the marsala or tea. Bring to the boil, then remove the pan from the heat and leave to stand until all the liquid has been absorbed by the figs.

Mix the flour, baking powder, mixed spice and breadcrumbs together and add a generous pinch of salt.

Beat the non-dairy spread and sugar together until well combined, then add the flour mixture, grated carrot, aquafaba and figs. Stir until thoroughly combined.

Grease a 750g pudding basin with non-dairy spread. Scrape the batter into the basin and smooth the top. Cover the basin with a piece of pleated foil and secure it firmly with a rubber band or string.

Stand the pudding in a steamer and place the steamer over a large saucepan of simmering water. Alternatively, fold up a small tea towel and put it in the base of a large saucepan. Place the pudding on top and add boiling water to about a third of the way up the basin. Steam the pudding for about 2 hours, keeping the water at simmering level and checking the water level regularly so the pan doesn't boil dry.

Remove the pudding from the steamer or saucepan and leave it to stand for 5 minutes. Remove the foil, run a palette knife around the edge of the pudding to loosen it, then turn it out on to a plate. Serve with custard.

350–400g ripe fresh apricots, halved and stoned

2 tbsp caster sugar

2 tbsp brandy

a few drops of almond extract (optional, be sparing)

softened butter, for greasing

1 tbsp demerara sugar

1 tbsp ground almonds

**Batter**

30g plain flour

30g ground almonds

30g caster sugar

zest of 1 orange

pinch of salt

2 eggs

300ml whole milk

30g butter, melted

a few drops of almond extract (optional)

**To finish**

icing sugar

# Apricot clafoutis

A traditional French pud, a clafoutis is made with fresh fruit baked in a light sponge mixture – and by golly, it's good. You can use lots of different types of fruit, but apricots are particularly delicious when they're in season. Use a shallow oven dish – a ceramic flan dish about 28cm in diameter is ideal.

Put the apricots in a bowl and sprinkle with the caster sugar. Add the brandy and the almond extract, if using, and leave the apricots to macerate for at least 2 hours – you can leave them overnight in the fridge if you like. Stir every so often to make sure they are all coated.

Preheat the oven to 180°C/Fan 160°C/Gas 4. Grease a large, shallow dish with butter. Mix the demerara sugar and ground almonds together, then sprinkle this over the butter.

To make the batter, mix the flour, ground almonds and sugar with the orange zest and a generous pinch of salt. Beat in the eggs, followed by the milk, melted butter and almond extract, if using, to make a smooth batter.

Arrange the apricots neatly in your dish, cut-side down, and then drizzle over any soaking liquid. Pour the batter around the apricots. Bake for 30–35 minutes, until the batter is a dappled golden brown and well puffed up. Remove from the oven, then dust with icing sugar and serve with cream, if you like.

MAKES 20

175g plain flour,
    plus extra for dusting

50g icing sugar

zest of 1 orange

pinch of salt

100g non-dairy spread, well chilled

2 tbsp aquafaba (liquid from a can
    of unsalted chickpeas)

3–4 tbsp jam

# Jammy dodgers

Si: this is for my vegan son James, who loves a jammy dodger.
It wasn't that easy but in the end, we've come up with the
goods and these are a great success, so fill your boots, son.
The dough is quite fragile, so you do need to follow the method
carefully and do just as we say! You'll thank us for it.

Put the flour and icing sugar into a bowl with the zest and a
generous pinch of salt. Mix, then add the non-dairy spread and
rub it in until the mixture resembles coarse breadcrumbs. Add
the aquafaba and combine until you have a smooth, soft dough.

Divide the dough into 4 pieces and knead lightly to make sure
each one is smooth and crack free. Wrap the dough in cling film
and freeze for 15–20 minutes. Preheat the oven to 160°C/Fan
140°C/Gas 3. Line 2 or 3 baking trays with baking paper.

Remove a piece of dough from the freezer. Generously dust your
work surface, rolling pin and the top of the dough with flour and
roll the dough out to a thickness of 3mm. Cut out 6cm rounds
and place them on a baking tray. Using a small cookie cutter (any
shape you like), cut out a small piece from the centre of half the
biscuits. Set aside any offcuts.

Repeat with the other 3 pieces of dough, kneading gently before
rolling. When you have used them all up, knead the offcuts
together until smooth – try not to work the dough too much.
Chill again before rolling out and cutting as before.

Bake for 10–12 minutes on the prepared trays – they won't take
on much colour on the top. Remove from the oven and leave to
cool and crisp up for a few minutes.

While still warm, spread about half a teaspoon of jam on the
bottom biscuits (the ones without the centre cut out), leaving a
½cm border all the way round. Place the biscuits with the centres
cut out on top. The jam should just spread to the edges but not
spill over. Leave to set.

SERVES 8

150g butter, softened, plus extra for greasing

125g golden caster sugar

zest of 2 medium oranges

pinch of salt

200g fine polenta

2 tsp baking powder

2 large eggs

**Syrup**

juice of 1 orange

juice of ½ lemon

100g icing sugar

**To serve (optional)**

2 tbsp icing sugar

a few drops of orange blossom water (optional)

200g thick crème fraiche or clotted cream

# Orange polenta cake

**Simple and delicious, this cake is made with polenta, not wheat flour, so ideal for anyone who needs a gluten-free teatime treat.**

Preheat the oven to 180°C/Fan 160°C/Gas 4. Grease the base and sides of a 20–21cm round cake tin with butter and line the base with baking paper.

Using an electric hand-held whisk or a stand mixer, cream the butter, sugar and orange zest together with a generous pinch of salt until very soft, light and increased in volume.

Mix the polenta with the baking powder. Add the eggs, one at a time, to the butter and sugar, adding 2 tablespoons of the polenta with each egg. Mix thoroughly after each addition, then gradually work in the rest of the polenta.

Scrape the mixture into your prepared tin and smooth the top with a spatula. Bake in the oven for about 35 minutes. When cooked, the cake will be springy to touch and will have shrunk away from the sides. It may sink a little in the middle, but this is perfectly normal.

To make the syrup, mix the juices and icing sugar together until the sugar has dissolved. While the cake is still hot and in its tin, pierce the top all over with a cocktail stick, then pour over the syrup as evenly as you can. Leave the cake to cool completely before removing it from the tin.

Stir the icing sugar and orange blossom water into the crème fraiche or clotted cream, if using, until well combined and serve on the side.

# Lemon bundt cake

cake-release spray or oil, for greasing

350g '00' plain flour, plus extra
for dusting

1 tbsp baking powder

1 tsp ground cardamom (optional)

200g caster sugar

pinch of salt

juice and zest of 2 lemons

100ml neutral vegetable oil
(avoid olive, unless very mild)

**Icing**

150g icing sugar

zest of 1 lemon

1 tbsp lemon juice

up to 1 tbsp plant-based milk

A bundt tin is ring-shaped with a hole in the middle, which helps you get a nice even bake. Bundt tins are usually moulded too, so you get a cake with a nice swirly pattern which looks dead professional. It is important to use '00' flour, often labelled for use in pasta and pizza, as it creates a fluffier, lighter cake than regular plain flour. Using oil in a cake mixture gives a nice moist texture and helps it keep well – if it gets the chance.

Preheat the oven to 170°C/Fan 150°C/Gas 3½. Prepare your bundt tin, spraying the inside with cake-release spray or rubbing it with oil and dusting it with flour. Make sure the surfaces are completely covered, including the centre, and that you remove any excess flour.

Mix the dry ingredients together along with a generous pinch of salt. Put the lemon juice in a jug and add enough tepid water to bring the amount of liquid up to 175ml. Mix in the lemon zest and oil, then pour this into the dry ingredients. Whisk to make a smooth batter.

Pour the batter into the prepared tin and bake in the oven for 40–45 minutes, until well risen and cooked through – a skewer or cocktail stick should come out clean. Leave the cake to cool in the tin for 5 minutes, then turn it out on to a cooling rack.

To make the icing, mix the icing sugar with the zest and lemon juice. Add enough milk to create a thick, smooth paste – it should be of a slow dropping consistency and will probably be thicker than you think it needs to be.

When the cake is cool, set the rack over a clean surface. Spoon the icing over the top, allowing it to slowly drip down the sides. Scoop up any icing which runs off and keep reapplying it until it is all used up. Cut into slices to serve.

# Banana tray bake

This really is epic. A sort of sticky upside-down banana cake, this ticks all the boxes for us. If you use a loose-bottomed tin just make sure you line it really well with baking paper or the sticky topping will ooze out. And that would be a crying shame. Magnificent with the coconut ice cream on page 220.

**Topping**

100g softened butter, plus extra for greasing

50g dark soft brown or muscovado sugar

50ml maple syrup

pinch of sea salt

zest and juice of 1 lime

2 bananas, each sliced into 3 lengthways

**Sponge**

300g self-raising flour

2 tsp baking powder

pinch of sea salt

225g softened butter

175g light soft brown sugar

50ml maple syrup

4 eggs

1 tsp vanilla extract

3 very ripe bananas, mashed

Preheat the oven to 180°C/Fan 160°C/Gas 4. Butter and line a 30 x 20cm baking tin with baking paper.

To make the topping, mix the 100g of butter, the 50g of sugar and 50ml of maple syrup together with a generous pinch of sea salt and the lime zest. When thoroughly combined, spread this mixture over the base of the baking tin in an even layer. Brush the banana slices with the lime juice (it is easier to brush rather than toss, as the slices will be fragile). Arrange them over the butter and sugar mixture in the tin.

To make the sponge, mix the flour with the baking powder and a pinch of salt. Beat the butter, sugar and syrup together until increased in volume and very soft. Add the eggs, one at a time, with a couple of tablespoons of the flour each time, mixing well in between. Add the remaining flour, the vanilla extract and mashed bananas and mix until well combined.

Scrape the mixture into the baking tin and spread evenly. Bake in the oven for 35–40 minutes until well risen and springy to touch. Remove from the oven and leave to cool in the tin for 10 minutes, then turn it out on to a plate or board and carefully remove the baking paper.

Serve warm with pouring cream or ice cream or leave to cool completely and cut into squares. Store in an airtight tin.

# Oatmeal chocolate chip cookies

225g porridge oats
125g plain flour
1 tsp bicarbonate of soda
½ tsp salt
125g non-dairy baking spread
100g light soft brown sugar
100g granulated sugar
2 tbsp golden syrup
2 tsp vanilla extract
2 tbsp plant-based milk
200g vegan chocolate chips or raisins

**Nothing like a good chunky cookie with your cup of tea and these are the business. Great with choc chips, of course, but they're also delicious with raisins when you want a change. If you're not vegan, you can use butter and ordinary milk instead of plant-based if you like.**

Preheat the oven to 180°C/Fan 160°C/Gas 4. Line 2 baking trays with baking paper.

Put the porridge oats in a food processor and pulse a few times – don't grind them to a flour, but they do need to be slightly broken up. Mix with the flour and bicarbonate of soda and add the salt.

Put the non-dairy spread and sugars into a bowl and beat with an electric hand-held whisk until soft and well aerated. Add the syrup, vanilla extract and milk, then beat again to combine.

Stir in the oat and flour mix and the chocolate chips or raisins to make a firm dough.

Scoop out balls of the dough, using a large spoon or ice cream scoop, and place them on the baking trays. Each ball should weigh about 45–50g. Make sure they are well spaced out on the trays, as they will spread.

Bake the cookies for 12–15 minutes until they are a rich golden brown. They will still be very soft in the middle. Remove from the oven and leave to cool completely on the baking trays before trying to move them – they will firm up as they cool. The texture should be crisp around the outside and chewy in the middle.

Store in an airtight container when cool.

# Dairy-free brownies

MAKES 12

cake-release spray (optional)
275ml plant-based milk
150ml groundnut or walnut oil
2 tsp vanilla extract
2 tbsp ground flax seeds
60ml hot water
125g plain flour
125g cocoa powder
½ tsp baking powder
100g light soft brown sugar
75g caster sugar
½ tsp salt
150g vegan chocolate chips
100g nut butter, any sort

No butter, no eggs – but these beauties still taste fantastic and swirling the nut butter in at the end is a great touch. We like to use peanut butter but almond or hazelnut are both fine too. There are lots of recipes for vegan brownies these days, but we think ours are the best we've tasted.

Preheat the oven to 180°C/Fan 160°C/Gas 4. Line a 20 x 20cm brownie tin with baking paper or spray with cake-release spray.

Whisk the milk, oil and vanilla extract together in a bowl and set aside. Mix the ground flax seeds with the hot water and leave to stand for 5 minutes. Whisk all the remaining ingredients, except the chocolate chips and the nut butter, together in a separate bowl.

Beat the flax seed mixture into the wet ingredients, then add the dry ingredients and fold them in as gently as you can. Add the chocolate chips and stir.

Scrape the mixture into the prepared tin. Dot spoonfuls of the nut butter all over the batter, then swirl it through, using the tip of a knife. Don't mix it up too much!

Bake for 20–25 minutes until the brownies have just set. Leave to cool completely, then cut into squares. If you want them extra fudgy, put them in the fridge for several hours. Otherwise transfer them to an airtight container.

SERVES 12

450g mixed dried fruit (raisins, sultanas, currants, blueberries, chopped apricots, chopped prunes)

75g glacé cherries, rinsed and halved

75g candied citrus peel, finely chopped

zest of 1 orange

75ml rum or brandy

225g plain flour

75g ground almonds

2 tsp mixed spice

1 tsp ground cinnamon

½ tsp bicarbonate of soda

½ tsp salt

150g dairy-free baking spread

100g soft dark brown sugar

50g soft light brown sugar

75ml almond or soya milk

1 tbsp cider vinegar

**To finish**

rum or brandy, for feeding

1 block of marzipan

3 tbsp apricot jam

75ml aquafaba (liquid from a can of unsalted chickpeas)

¼ tsp cream of tartar

300g icing sugar

lemon juice (if needed)

# Vegan Christmas cake

**This is a really fruity, delicious Christmas cake – but contains no eggs or butter, so it's fine if you're vegan and is great for everyone. You can leave it just as it is or go the whole hog and add marzipan and icing, then lots of decorations! That's Christmas sorted.**

Put all the fruit, including the cherries, citrus peel and citrus zests, into a bowl and pour over the rum or brandy. Leave to stand, stirring regularly, for several hours, or overnight.

Preheat the oven to 150°C/Fan 130°C/Gas 2. Line a deep 20cm round cake tin with baking paper and wrap a triple layer of foil around the outside. This will prevent the cake from burning around the edges during the long bake time.

Mix the flour with the ground almonds, spices and bicarbonate of soda. Add the salt and stir thoroughly.

Cream the dairy-free spread and sugars together – this is easiest done in a stand mixer or with an electric hand-held whisk. Add the flour mixture and the milk and vinegar, then stir to combine. Stir in the fruit, including any liquid left in the bowl.

Scrape the mixture into your prepared tin. Bake in the oven for 1½– 2 hours, until a skewer comes out clean and the internal temperature of the cake is 98°C. Cover the top of the cake with foil (this will help keep it soft) and leave to cool in the tin.

If you have made the cake well in advance, wrap it in plenty of baking paper and store it in an airtight container. Feed regularly with more rum or brandy. To do this, prick the underside of the cake all over with a skewer and pour over a tablespoon or two of the rum or brandy. Do this at least a couple of times in the run-up to Christmas.

To decorate, roll out the marzipan until it's large enough to cover the top and sides of the cake. If the top of the cake is uneven, shave some off so it's completely flat, then upturn the cake, so the bottom becomes the top – this will give you a much cleaner finish. Warm the jam through, then brush it generously over the cake. Cover the cake with the marzipan and leave to dry out overnight.

To make the royal icing, whisk the aquafaba with the cream of tartar until it has frothed up but is nowhere near soft peaks (you don't want it too aerated). Add the sugar all at once and stir until it has completely combined. To coat the cake, it needs to be a reluctant dropping consistency – add a few drops of lemon juice to thin it if necessary or a little more icing sugar if you want it thicker.

Pour the icing over the cake and smooth it with a palette knife. For a rough snow scene, use a palette knife to form little peaks all over the top. Or, if you prefer, make it as smooth as you can by dipping the palette knife in just-boiled water and dragging it over the icing in a circular motion. Leave the icing to set, then add any extra decorations you like.

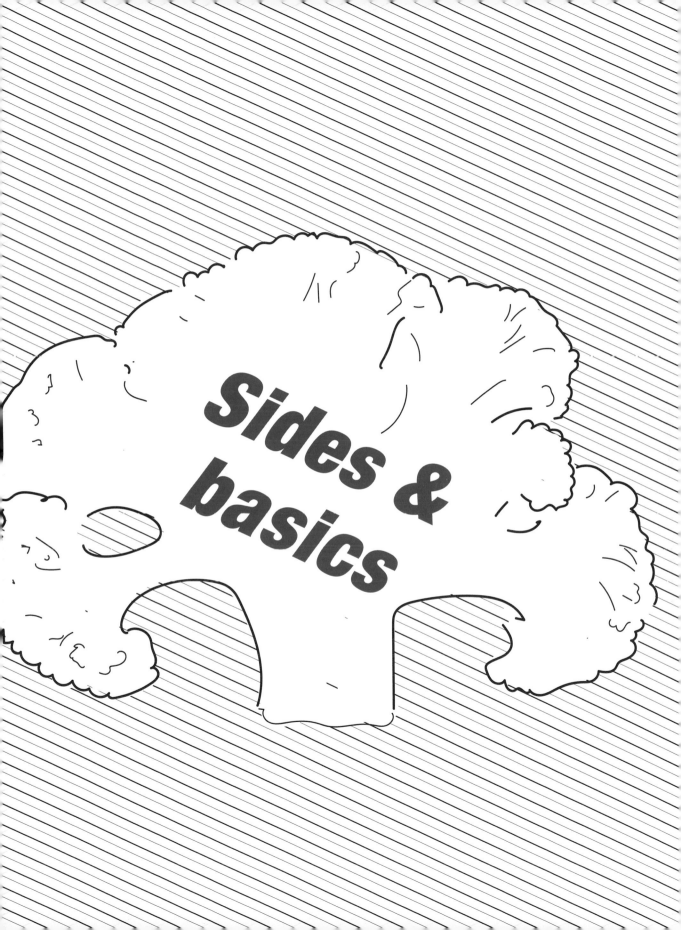

Sides &
basics

Roast potatoes & parsnips 250

Dauphinoise potatoes 251

Boulangère potatoes 252

Home-made baked beans 253

A quick dal 254

Root vegetable purées 255

Carrot & swede purée 256

Cauliflower rice 256

Sautéed greens 257

Roast cabbage 258

Caramelised endive 258

Quick tomato relish 259

Fermented tomatoes 260

Vegan cream sauce 262

Raita 262

Tomato sauce 263

Vegan custard 264

Tamago eggs 265

Tofu bacon 266

Biker spice mix 266

Gyoza wrappers 267

Shortcrust pastry 268

Vegan pastry 268

How to cook chickpeas 270

How to cook quinoa 271

Cooking rice 272

How to cook black beans 274

Basic vegetable stock 276

Mushroom stock 277

SERVES 4–6

# Roast potatoes & parsnips

1kg floury potatoes (such as Maris Pipers), peeled and cut into large chunks (reserve peelings)

600g parsnips, peeled and cut into large chunks

2 tbsp fine semolina or polenta

75ml olive oil

a few sprigs of rosemary (optional)

sea salt and black pepper

**Proper crispy roasties are a must with the Christmas veggie Wellington on page 206.**

Preheat the oven to 200°C/Fan 180°C/Gas 6.

Bring a large pan of water to the boil and add plenty of salt. Wrap the reserved peelings in a piece of muslin and tie into a bundle – they really add flavour, as there is so much in the skins. Add the bundle to the pan along with the potatoes and the parsnips. Boil for 5–6 minutes until the potatoes and parsnips start to soften around the edges.

Drain thoroughly, discard the peelings, then return the veg to the pan. Cover the pan with a tea towel and leave over a very low heat for a few minutes to get the potatoes and parsnips really dry. Then put the lid on and give the pan a good shake. This will rough up the edges of the veg and help them crisp up. Sprinkle with the fine semolina or polenta.

Pour the olive oil into a large roasting tin and place the tin in the oven for a couple of minutes to heat up. Carefully add the potatoes and parsnips when the oil is hot. Season with plenty of salt and pepper and tuck in the sprigs of rosemary, if using. Roast for 40–45 minutes until crisp and browned on the outside and very fluffy within.

# Dauphinoise potatoes

**A deliciously luxurious side dish, this is also lovely served on its own with salad.**

---

Preheat the oven to 180°C/Fan 160°C/Gas 4.

Rub a shallow gratin dish with the cut halves of garlic, then take a small piece of the butter and rub this around the dish as well.

Rinse the potatoes to get rid of excess starch, then dry them as thoroughly as you can. Layer them in the gratin dish, seasoning with salt and pepper as you go.

Put the double cream and milk in a jug and whisk in the flour. This helps stop the cream curdling. Pour the mixture over the potatoes, then dot the remaining butter on top. Grate over a little nutmeg, if using.

Bake for an hour, then turn the heat up to 220°C/Fan 200°C/Gas 7 and bake for a further 10 minutes or until the top layer of potatoes has turned a crisp golden brown.

1 garlic clove, cut in half

25g butter

1kg salad/waxy potatoes (such as Charlottes), thinly sliced

300ml double cream

400ml whole milk

1 tsp plain flour

grating of nutmeg (optional)

sea salt and black pepper

# Boulangère potatoes

2 tbsp olive oil, plus extra for greasing

1 large onion, thinly sliced

3–4 sprigs of fresh thyme, plus extra to garnish

3 garlic cloves, thinly sliced

1.2kg floury potatoes (such as Maris Pipers), thinly sliced to the thickness of a £1 coin

400ml vegetable stock

sea salt and black pepper

**This is a lighter potato dish than the dauphinoise, but it's still really good and is suitable for a vegan meal.**

Heat the oil in a large non-stick frying pan. Add the onion and thyme sprigs and fry gently, stirring occasionally, for 8–10 minutes, until the onion has softened and browned slightly. Add the garlic and continue to fry for 2–3 minutes, then season to taste with sea salt and black pepper.

Preheat the oven to 200°C/Fan 180°C/Gas 6. Grease a 20 x 30cm roasting tin or ovenproof dish with a little oil. Arrange a layer of potato slices over the base of the dish. Sprinkle over a third of the fried onions. Continue layering the potato slices and onion mixture, ending with a layer of potatoes.

Pour over the stock until it just reaches the top layer of potatoes. Season again with black pepper and garnish with a few sprigs of thyme. Bake for about 1 hour and 15 minutes or until the potatoes are tender and lovely and brown on top.

# Home-made baked beans

We've all got a can of baked beans in the cupboard, but making your own with dried beans is great for taste and saves loads of money. A bag of 500g of dried beans costs not much more than a one can of beans and gives you about 1.3–1.5kg of cooked! These are great for the fry-up on page 20 and for topping baked potatoes (see page 138).

500g haricot beans, soaked
   overnight and drained

1 onion, left whole

5 cloves

2 bay leaves

sprig of parsley

2 tbsp olive oil

1 onion, finely chopped

3 garlic cloves, finely chopped

1 tsp garlic powder

400g can of tomatoes, puréed

2 tsp Dijon mustard

1 tbsp black treacle

1 tbsp light soft brown sugar

1 tsp Marmite

dash of mushroom ketchup

dash of liquid smoke (optional)

sea salt and black pepper

Put the soaked beans in a large saucepan, cover with fresh water and add a teaspoon of salt. Stud the onion with the cloves and add it to the pot along with the bay leaves and parsley. Bring to the boil, then turn the heat down slightly and simmer the beans for an hour. By this time, they should be almost tender but still keeping their shape.

Strain the beans, reserving the cooking liquor. Heat the oil in the pan and add the chopped onion. Cook gently until translucent, then turn up the heat and allow the onion to caramelise around the edges. Add the garlic and cook for another couple of minutes, then stir in the garlic powder.

Pour in the tomatoes and tip the beans back into the pan. Add just enough of the cooking liquor to cover the beans, bring to the boil, then turn the heat down to a simmer. Stir in the mustard, black treacle, sugar, Marmite and mushroom ketchup. Taste and add salt to taste and black pepper. Continue to cook, partially covered with a lid, until the sauce has thickened and the beans are tender. Taste for seasoning and adjust as necessary. Add a few drops of the liquid smoke if you like – be careful with this as it can easily overpower the flavour.

The baked beans will keep for a week in the fridge or can be frozen in portions.

1 tbsp vegetable oil

3 garlic cloves, crushed

15g fresh root ginger, grated

½ tsp ground turmeric

½ tsp ground cinnamon

½ tsp ground cumin

½ tsp ground coriander

½ tsp ground cardamom

a pinch of asafoetida

200g lentils (any split sort or mung beans), well rinsed

sea salt and black pepper

**Garnish (optional)**

1 tbsp vegetable oil

1 tsp mustard seeds

12 curry leaves

a few coriander leaves, to serve

a few green chillies, chopped, to serve

# A quick dal

**This can be served on its own in a bowl, as a side dish or with rice. Very versatile! You don't have to add all the spices if you don't want to, but we always use at least a pinch of turmeric and a pinch of asafoetida.**

Heat the oil in a large saucepan and add the garlic, ginger and spices, if using. Stir to combine and cook for a couple of minutes. Stir in the dal and then add a litre of water. Season with plenty of salt and pepper, then bring to the boil and turn the heat down to a simmer. Cook until the dal is tender – this will take anything from 20 minutes for red lentils to up to 40 minutes for firmer varieties.

For the garnish, if using, heat the oil in a small frying pan and add the mustard seeds and curry leaves. When the mustard seeds start popping and the curry leaves look dry and start to crackle, remove the pan from the heat and pour the mixture over the dal. Serve sprinkled with coriander leaves and green chillies.

# Root vegetable purées

We think that some root vegetables, such as celeriac, parsnips, sweet potatoes and Jerusalem artichokes, are best puréed with a bit of potato in the mix.

Serves 4

500g celeriac, parsnips, sweet potatoes or Jerusalem artichokes, diced

250g floury potatoes, diced

50ml whole milk, warmed through

25g butter

2 tsp wholegrain mustard (optional)

herbs (optional)

sea salt and black pepper

Bring a large saucepan of water to the boil and add a generous amount of salt. Add whichever root vegetables you choose and the potatoes, then simmer until they are very tender.

Drain thoroughly and tip the veg back into the pan. Cover with a tea towel and leave the pan over a very low heat for 5 minutes, shaking the pan every so often, to dry the vegetables out.

Put the veg through a potato ricer or use a regular masher – don't be tempted to use a stick blender, as it will make the potatoes go gluey. Season again with salt and pepper, then add the milk and butter. Add mustard, if using – it does go very well with celeriac and Jerusalem artichokes. Mix thoroughly and keep the purée warm until served.

If you want to add herbs to the mash, take small bunches and separate leaves from stems. Use any herbs you like, but sage works particularly well with parsnips and Jerusalem artichokes; thyme with celeriac and sweet potato; and parsley with sweet potato.

Add the stems to the cooking water and discard them when you drain the vegetables. Finely chop the leaves. Melt the butter and add the leaves. Swirl the herbs around in the butter or oil before stirring them through the mashed vegetables.

 **BIKER VEGAN TIP**

To make vegan root veg purées, use plant-based milk instead of regular, and a tablespoon of olive oil instead of butter.

75g butter
1 swede, cut into small dice (2–3cm)
3 large carrots, diced
sea salt and white pepper

# Carrot & swede purée

**These veg are best without potato in the mix and this purée goes really well with vegetarian haggis. If you want to make this recipe vegan, use non-dairy spread instead of butter. Oil doesn't work well here.**

Melt the butter in a lidded saucepan and add the swede and carrots. Season with plenty of salt and white pepper. Cook over a medium-high heat, stirring frequently, until you start to see liquid appear in the base of the pan.

Cover and cook at a very gentle simmer for 40–45 minutes until the vegetables are completely tender and have reduced a bit in volume. Blend to a purée or roughly crush and stir to get the benefit of the pan juices.

about 500g cauliflower
1 tbsp olive oil
sea salt and black pepper

# Cauliflower rice

**This is a great way of using up the rest of the cauliflower if you make the cauliflower steaks on page 140. It soaks up juices beautifully and it's very low in calories, so good if you're watching your weight.**

Divide the cauliflower into florets and put them, stalks and all, into a food processor. Blitz to the texture of fine breadcrumbs.

Heat the olive oil in a large frying pan. Add the cauliflower and stir for a few minutes, then season with salt and pepper. Add about 100ml of water and cook over a medium heat for about 5 minutes, stirring frequently, until the water has been absorbed. The cauliflower should be tender but still with a little bite to it.

If you like, you can add chopped fresh herbs, fried onions, flaked almonds or spices to the cauliflower.

# Sautéed greens

SERVES 4

You can prepare any fairly robust greens, such as cabbage, spring greens, kale and sprout tops, in this way. This also works well with chard but it won't need to cook for so long.

Heat the olive oil and butter in a large sauté pan. When the butter has started to foam, add the onion and cook gently until soft and translucent. Add the garlic, if using, and cook for a further 2 minutes, then add the cabbage or greens. Season with salt and pepper.

Fry, stirring frequently, until the cabbage has started to reduce down in volume but is still crisp. Add a splash of water and continue to cook until the cabbage is al dente or softer, depending on your preference. Add the nutmeg, chilli or zest, if using, then stir in the parsley leaves.

1 tbsp olive oil

15g butter

1 small onion, finely chopped

2 garlic cloves, finely chopped (optional)

600g cabbage or other greens, finely shredded

a few rasps of nutmeg (optional)

a generous pinch of chilli flakes (optional)

zest of ½ lemon or lime (optional)

a few parsley leaves, finely chopped

sea salt and black pepper

SERVES 4

1 cabbage (any sort) cut into 8–12
   wedges, depending on size

3 tbsp olive oil

sea salt and black pepper

# Roast cabbage

**This is great on its own as a side, but for a quick supper or lunch dish it can be dressed with any salad dressing or a sprinkling of herbs and spices. Another option is to top it with a mixture of breadcrumbs, herbs and cheese for the last 10 minutes of the cooking time.**

Preheat the oven to 200°C/Fan 180°C/Gas 6. Arrange the cabbage wedges in a roasting tin and drizzle over the olive oil. Massage the oil into the cabbage, making sure all the surfaces are covered, then season with salt and pepper.

Roast for about 40 minutes. The core of the cabbage wedges should be tender when you pierce them with a knife and the edges will have crisped up and browned.

SERVES 4

1 tbsp honey or maple syrup
   (optional)

4 heads of red or white endive,
   trimmed and halved lengthways

2 tbsp olive oil

30g butter

100ml white wine

leaves from a large sprig of thyme

sea salt and black pepper

# Caramelised endive

**This is good as it is or for a treat, cover the caramelised endive in béchamel sauce and cheese and bake in the oven.**

If using honey or maple syrup, heat it very gently in a small saucepan, then brush it over the cut sides of the endives.

Heat the oil in a wide frying pan. When it is hot, add the endives, cut-side down. Cook for several minutes until the undersides have developed a good caramel colour, then turn over and continue to cook for several more minutes. Season with salt and pepper.

Add the butter. As soon as it starts to foam, add the white wine and the thyme. Bring to the boil, then turn down the heat and simmer until the liquid has reduced to a syrupy consistency and the endives are completely tender.

# Quick tomato relish

**This is easy to make and it goes down a treat with the cheese, potato and onion pasties on page 116. Great in a sandwich too.**

Heat a cast-iron pan or any flameproof pan (it's best to avoid pans with a non-stick coating). Cut the tomatoes in half and scoop out the seeds. Place the tomatoes, skin-side down, in the pan and cook until the skin has charred in patches. Flip over to caramelise the cut sides, then remove the tomatoes from the pan and roughly chop them.

Add the olive oil to the pan, followed by the red onion. Cook gently over a medium high heat until the onion has browned, but still has plenty of crunch. Stir in the garlic and thyme. Season with plenty of salt and pepper and put the tomatoes back in the pan.

Add the sugar and vinegar. Bring to the boil very briefly – the tomatoes should break down quickly – then remove the pan from the heat and stir in the olives and chilli flakes. While the relish is still warm, taste for seasoning and add more sugar, vinegar, chilli or salt to get the flavour you like. It should have a sharp, sweet and sour taste.

Tip the relish into a bowl and leave to cool, then store in the fridge for up to a week.

500g ripe tomatoes
2 tbsp olive oil
1 large red onion, finely chopped
2 garlic cloves, crushed
leaves from a sprig of thyme
1 tsp sugar
2 tbsp cider or sherry vinegar
50g green olives, pitted and sliced
1 tsp chilli flakes
sea salt and black pepper

MAKES 1 JAR

200g cherry tomatoes
3 bay leaves
a few peppercorns
5g sea salt
200ml spring water
a piece of cabbage

# Fermented tomatoes

**Quick and easy to prepare, these make a nice little side dish and are just the thing with the tattie scones on page 24. It is important to use spring water, as the chlorine in tap water inhibits the right bacteria from forming. And make sure the tomatoes you use aren't too ripe.**

Wash and dry the tomatoes and bay leaves thoroughly. Put them in a sterilised 450g jar with the peppercorns – there should still be plenty of space at the top. Dissolve the salt in the spring water.

Fold up the piece of cabbage to fit the jar and put it on top of the tomatoes. This will act as a weight and stop the tomatoes from rising above the water. Pour in the water, making sure there are no air bubbles and that the water comes just above the cabbage, so you can be sure the tomatoes are under water.

Loosely close the lid and leave the jar somewhere dark at room temperature. Check every day and loosen the lid to prevent gases from building up. After 24 hours you should see a few bubbles appear. After another day there should be many more around the tomatoes and on the surface of the water.

Leave for 2–4 days, checking every day until the tomatoes smell pleasantly sour. At this point, transfer the jar to the fridge. The tomatoes will continue to ferment at a much slower rate and can now be eaten. They will keep in the fridge for several months.

125g unsalted cashew nuts
1 tsp cider vinegar
1 tsp lime juice
1 tbsp nutritional yeast (optional)
pinch of salt

# Vegan cream sauce

**This is a useful vegan sauce and can also make a good base for dips. We've made the nutritional yeast optional, as not everyone likes it, but it does add some extra savouriness to the sauce.**

Soak the cashew nuts overnight in a bowl with plenty of water. Alternatively, cover them with boiling water and leave them to stand for at least an hour.

Drain the nuts and put them in a blender with all the other ingredients and 125ml of water. Blend at a high speed for at least 5 minutes, stopping at regular intervals to scrape down the sides, until you have a smooth creamy paste. If you find there are still a few resistant flecks of nuts, push the mixture through a fine sieve. Taste for seasoning and adjust as you like. This will keep in the fridge for at least a week and will also freeze.

For a garlic sauce, add a teaspoon of finely chopped garlic to the blender with the other ingredients. This is really good for using in the Mexican buddha bowl recipe on page 38.

# Raita

250g yoghurt (plain or plant-based)
2 tsp dried mint
½ tsp sugar
1 tsp white wine vinegar
sea salt

**Serve this with the vegetable biryani on page 184 or with any of the curries. Use a plant-based yoghurt for a vegan raita.**

Simply mix the yoghurt, mint, sugar and vinegar together in a bowl and season with plenty of salt.

# Tomato sauce

This is a good basic sauce for use in dishes such as lasagne (see page 178) and the stuffed pasta shells (see page 194). For the pasta shells, it's best to use fresh tomatoes if possible.

1kg fresh, ripe tomatoes, peeled and chopped or 2 x 400g cans of tomatoes

3 tbsp olive oil

1 onion, very finely chopped

4 garlic cloves, very finely chopped

1 tsp dried oregano or 1 sprig of fresh, left whole

basil leaves

sea salt and black pepper

If using fresh tomatoes, remove the cores if they are particularly big and score a cross in the base. Put the tomatoes in a bowl, cover them with boiling water and leave to stand for about 10 seconds. Drain and then peel – the skins should just slip off very ripe tomatoes. Roughly chop. If you have a high-powered blender, you can just blend the tomatoes until absolutely smooth – no need to peel first.

Heat the olive oil in a large saucepan. Add the onion and sprinkle with salt, then cook gently over a low heat until very soft and translucent. Turn up the heat slightly, add the garlic and continue to cook for a couple of minutes. Add the tomatoes and oregano, then season again with salt and pepper.

Bring the sauce to the boil, then turn down to a simmer and cover the pan. Cook for about half an hour, then remove the lid and continue to simmer until the sauce has reduced by just under about a third.

Add a few basil leaves and leave to simmer for another few minutes, just to infuse a little flavour, then remove the basil and the whole oregano sprig, if used. Remove from the heat.

The sauce will keep in the fridge for up to a week and can also be frozen in portions.

500ml plant-based milk

1 vanilla pod, split lengthways

2 tbsp caster sugar

3 tbsp cornflour or custard powder

# Vegan custard

**Lovely with the figgy pudding on page 228.**

Put 400ml of the milk into a saucepan with the vanilla and sugar. Warm through, stirring to dissolve the sugar, until the milk is close to boiling. Remove from the heat.

Mix the cornflour or custard powder with the remaining milk to make a smooth, runny paste. Gradually pour the warm milk on to this mixture, stirring constantly as you do so, then pour the mixture back into the pan.

Cook over a medium heat, stirring constantly, until the custard thickens to a pouring consistency. Whisk to make sure it is lump free, then pour it into a jug and serve.

# Tamago eggs

MAKES 4

**These marinated eggs can be added to the ramen on page 74.**

4 large eggs
150ml soy sauce
3 tbsp mirin or rice wine
2 tbsp rice wine vinegar
3 garlic cloves, crushed
1 tsp chilli flakes

Bring a saucepan of water to the boil and carefully lower in the eggs. Turn down the heat to a simmer and cook the eggs for 6 minutes, then remove them from the heat and run them under cold water. Peel the eggs.

Put the soy sauce in a saucepan with the mirin or rice wine and the vinegar. Add 300ml of water, the garlic and chilli flakes. Bring to the boil, then turn down and simmer for 5 minutes.

Put the eggs in a deep, narrow container, then pour over the soy mixture – it should completely cover the eggs. Leave for at least an hour before using, gently shaking the container every so often to ensure even coverage.

1 tbsp olive oil

1 tbsp maple syrup

1 tbsp tamari or soy sauce

½ tsp garlic powder

½ tsp onion granules

¼ tsp annatto powder

a few drops of liquid smoke (optional)

100g smoked tofu, very finely diced
  or thinly sliced

sea salt and black pepper

# Tofu bacon

Clever flavouring can give tofu a satisfyingly bacon-like flavour. For recipes such as the American-style layered salad (see page 58), dice the tofu to make bacon bits. For the tofu scramble (see page 20), cut the tofu into thin slices.

Heat the olive oil in a frying pan and add all the other ingredients. Stir until the tofu is completely coated, then season with salt and pepper. Fry the tofu over a medium heat, stirring regularly, until the tofu is crisp – this will take several minutes.

Remove the tofu from the heat and spread it out on kitchen paper to dry. It will continue to crisp up as it cools. When cool, transfer it to a container and keep it in the fridge for up to a week.

1 tsp each of ground turmeric, cumin
  and coriander

½ tsp each of ground cinnamon,
  cardamom, fenugreek and white
  pepper

chilli powder, to taste

# Biker spice mix

A great spice mix for the keema peas recipe on page 144 or whenever you need a good spicy flavour for a dish.

Mix everything, except the chilli powder, together in a bowl. Then add the chilli powder – a small amount if you want a mild mix, more if you like your food hot, hot, hot.

# Gyoza wrappers

MAKES 24

**You can buy these in Asian supermarkets but if you are making potstickers (see page 100), you might like to make your own.**

75g strong white flour

75g plain flour, plus extra for dusting

75ml just-boiled water

½ tsp salt

Put the flours into a bowl. Mix the just-boiled water with the salt, then add this to the flour, mixing it in with a knife. It will seem very floury to start with but keep going and it will come together. Don't be tempted to add more water. Cover with a damp cloth for 10 minutes, then remove and knead until the dough is smooth and elastic. Cover the dough again and leave it to stand somewhere warm for an hour.

Cut the dough into 2 equal pieces and dust your work surface with flour. Roll the dough out as thinly as you can. It will be resistant to start with, but you will eventually end up with a round about 35cm in diameter and with a thickness of less than 1mm.

Cut the dough into rounds using a 9cm cutter, then repeat with the other piece of dough. Knead the offcuts together and roll again. You should end up with at least 24 discs. Dust with flour in between each one if you want to stack them together.

SERVES 4

250g plain flour
½ tsp salt
125g butter, chilled and diced
1 egg, beaten

# Shortcrust pastry

**Use this for the leek and goat's cheese tart on page 168 and for the galette on page 182.**

Put the flour into a bowl with the salt. Add the butter and rub it in until the mixture resembles fine breadcrumbs. Add the egg and stir to combine, then add just enough iced water to bind the dough together – a tablespoon should be enough. Wrap the dough in cling film and then put it in the fridge to chill for half an hour before using.

SERVES 4

150g plain flour
½ tsp baking powder
½ tsp salt
75g non-dairy spread, chilled
and cubed

# Vegan pastry

**Use this for the vegan plate pie on page 148.**

To make the pastry, put the flour and baking powder into a bowl and add the salt. Rub in the non-dairy spread, then add just enough iced water to bring the dough together. Wrap the dough in cling film, then put it in the fridge to chill for at least half an hour before using.

500g chickpeas
sea salt

# How to cook chickpeas

**Chickpeas take longer to cook than any other pulses, but this method can be adapted for other beans, just with reduced cooking times. It is impossible to give really accurate timings because chickpeas vary enormously in size and age – the older they are, the longer they will take. As they do take so long, it's a good idea to cook 500g at a time, then freeze them. Cooked chickpeas freeze really well.**

Cover the chickpeas in plenty of cold water, then leave them for at least 8 hours, preferably overnight. If you want to speed this up a bit, you can do a 'quick' soak. Put the chickpeas straight into a saucepan, cover them with water and bring to the boil for one minute. Remove from the heat and leave to stand for an hour.

Drain the chickpeas (regardless of how you have soaked them) and cover them with fresh water. Make sure they have at least 5cm of water over them. Bring to the boil and boil fiercely for about 5 minutes, then add a teaspoon of salt and reduce the temperature to a gentle simmer. Cook for at least 45 minutes, gently stirring now and then just to move them around.

Check to see if they are cooked – they can take longer, anything up to an hour and a half, depending on age. If they aren't quite cooked, continue to check every 10–15 minutes.

When you are happy that the chickpeas are cooked, drain and store them in the fridge or freezer. You can use the cooking liquid as stock for soup.

# How to cook quinoa

**Quinoa is great in a salad (see page 38) and also makes a great side dish. You can just boil quinoa in water, but this method gives much better and tastier results.**

200g quinoa

1 tsp coconut oil or 1 tbsp olive oil

300ml vegetable stock or water

1 bay leaf

small bunch of coriander (optional)

sea salt

Put the quinoa into a sieve and wash it thoroughly under a cold tap for at least 30 seconds – this will help remove its coating (saponin), which can make the quinoa taste soapy. Transfer the quinoa to a bowl and cover with water. Leave to soak for 5 minutes, then drain thoroughly.

Heat the oil in a saucepan and add the quinoa. Fry the quinoa, stirring regularly, for several minutes. There will be some steam at first – this is from any liquid left on the quinoa. Keep frying until the quinoa starts to smell nutty – it may also start popping.

Add the stock or water and the bay leaf, then season with salt. If using coriander, separate the leaves from the stems and finely chop both. Add the stems to the pan.

Bring to the boil, then turn down the heat to a low simmer and cover. Cook for 12 minutes, then remove from the heat and leave to stand for 5–7 minutes. During this time the quinoa will continue to steam and become drier. If using the coriander, add the finely chopped leaves, then fluff up everything together with a fork. Serve hot or cold.

SERVES 4–6

300g long-grain rice
1 tsp salt

# Cooking rice

**This basic absorption method works for basmati and jasmine rice – any long-grain rice that isn't the easy-cook variety. Aromatics can be added at the beginning of this process – whole spices work best if you aren't using any oil. You can also heat a tablespoon of oil at the beginning and gently cook any combination of onion, garlic and ginger before continuing as the method below.**

---

Rinse the rice in cold water until it is no longer cloudy, then drain thoroughly. Put it in a pan and heat gently to steam off the excess water – this also toasts the rice to give it a slightly nuttier flavour.

Pour in 450ml of water and add the salt. Bring to the boil, then turn the heat down. Put a folded tea towel or several layers of kitchen paper over the top of the pan and place the lid on top. Simmer for about 15 minutes until all the liquid has been absorbed, then remove the pan from the heat and leave the rice to stand for a further 10 minutes until perfectly dry. Fluff the rice up with a fork.

# Lemon or lime rice

Add a few pieces of pared zest to the rice at the start of the cooking time.

# Coriander rice

Take a small bunch of coriander and separate the leaves from the stems. Finely chop the coriander stems and add them to the pan with the rice. Blitz half the leaves with some of the water you are going to use for the rice and add this to the rice with the rest of the water. Finely chop the remaining leaves and fork them through once the rice has finished standing.

# Coconut rice

Add 50g of powdered coconut milk to the rice before adding the water – this makes for a less oily rice than using coconut milk. Alternatively, replace 100ml of the water with 100ml of coconut cream.

# Rice & peas

Add coconut milk to the rice as above, adding a sprig of thyme and half a teaspoon of allspice berries as well. Season with black pepper as well as salt.

The 'peas' in this Caribbean-style recipe are actually kidney beans. Take a can of drained and rinsed red kidney beans and add them to the rice, then cook as for the basic recipe opposite.

# How to cook black beans

500g dried black beans

vegetable stock or water, to cover

1 small can of coconut cream (optional)

bouquet garni (2 slices of onion, 2 cloves, 3 bay leaves, 1 tsp allspice berries and a sprig of thyme, all tied together in a muslin bag)

1 tsp sea salt

You'll need black beans for the tacos on page 172, but other beans can be cooked in much the same way as the method below, although they might need longer or shorter cooking times. You may be surprised to see that we add salt to the beans while cooking – the thing about only adding salt at the end is actually an old wives' tale! The beans will be more tender and creamier if salt is added at the start. A 500g bag of black beans makes about 1.2kg of cooked beans.

First soak the beans overnight. If you don't have time to do this, you can quick soak them instead. Simply cover the beans with water, bring to the boil and fast boil them for one minute. Then cover and leave to stand for an hour. This will give you the equivalent of overnight soaking.

Drain the beans and add stock or fresh water to cover, adding in the coconut cream, if using. Add the bouquet garni and salt. Bring to the boil, then turn down the heat and leave to simmer for at least an hour, stirring every so often. The beans might take longer, depending on how old they are. When they are tender, drain, reserving the cooking liquid if you like to use as a stock, and discard the bouquet garni.

These beans should keep in the fridge for a week, or in the freezer for at least a year.

# Basic vegetable stock

1 tsp olive oil

2 large onions, roughly chopped,

3 large carrots, chopped

200g squash or pumpkin, unpeeled, diced

4 celery sticks, sliced

2 leeks, sliced

100ml white wine or vermouth

a large sprig of thyme

a large sprig of parsley

1 bay leaf

a few peppercorns

**A good stock will make all the difference to your dishes, so it's well worth making a big batch and storing it in the freezer.**

Heat the olive oil in a large saucepan. Add all the vegetables and fry them over a high heat, stirring regularly, until they're starting to brown and caramelise around the edges. This will take at least 10 minutes. Add the white wine or vermouth and boil until it has evaporated away.

Cover the veg with 2 litres of water and add the herbs and peppercorns. Bring to the boil, then turn the heat down to a gentle simmer. Cook the stock, uncovered, for about an hour, stirring every so often.

Check the stock – the colour should have some depth to it. Strain it through a colander or a sieve lined with muslin, kitchen paper or coffee filter paper into a bowl and store it in the fridge for up to a week. Alternatively, pour the stock into freezer-proof containers and freeze.

# Mushroom stock

Use this stock for dishes such as the mushroom risotto (see page 188) and the mushroom bourguignon (see page 180) for a good rich flavour.

Make the stock as for the basic recipe on page 276, but add the mushrooms and garlic at the beginning. Once the vegetables are well browned, add the tomato purée and mushroom ketchup. Stir them into the vegetables, then proceed as for the basic stock.

To make stronger, earthier stock, soak 15g of dried mushrooms in water and add these and the soaking liquid with the water.

MAKES ABOUT 1.5 LITRES

ingredients as for basic vegetable stock (see p.276)

100g mushrooms, thinly sliced

2 garlic cloves, sliced

1 tbsp tomato purée

1 tsp mushroom ketchup

# Index

## A

**almond milk** 11
Almond rice pudding & cherry compote 216
Coffee crème brûlée 218
Pasta with creamy black pepper sauce 134

**almonds** 9
Almond rice pudding & cherry compote 216
Apricot clafoutis 230
Stuffed pasta shells 194
Tamari almonds 106
American-style layered salad 58
American-style pancakes 30

**apples**
Roast beetroot, goat's cheese & apple salad 36
Spicy baked apples 226
Apricot clafoutis 230

**aquafaba**
Jammy dodgers 232
Summer berries pavlova 224
Vegan chocolate mousse 214

**artichokes/artichoke hearts**
Artichoke & fennel paella 204
Artichoke & basil dip 102
Couscous-stuffed peppers 128
Vegan pizzas 198

**asparagus** 9
Asparagus mimosa 54
Summer vegetable soup 80

## B

**aubergines**
Aubergine katsu 176
Caribbean-style vegetable soup 84
Roasted aubergine pasta 150
Spaghetti & 'meatballs' 130
Vegan sausage rolls 98–9

**avocados** 9
Guacamole 172

Baked beans, Home-made 253

**bakes**
Chilli bean bake 156
Mediterranean-style vegetable bake 152
*see also* tray bakes
Banana tray bake 238
Barbecue sauce & sausages 200

**barley**
Brussels sprout & chestnut barley risotto 124

**basil**
Artichoke & basil dip 102
Batter 230

**beans** *see* black, borlotti, broad, butter, cannellini, edamame, green, haricot, kidney, pinto and runner beans

**bean sprouts**
Chow mein 140
Béchamel sauce 178

**beetroot**
Roast beetroot, goat's cheese & apple salad 36
Root vegetable tray bake 136
Winter vegetable soup with dumplings 64
Bhajis, Pickled onion 112
Biker blinis 95
Biker burgers 196
Biker spice mix 266
Biryani, Vegetable 184–5

**black beans** 9, 274
Biker burgers 196
Black bean & chipotle tacos 172
Mexican buddha bowl 38

**Blackberries** 9
Summer berries pavlova 224
Blinis, Biker 95
BLT sandwiches, vegan-style 118, 266

**blueberries**
Summer berries pavlova 224

**borlotti beans** 9
Pasta & bean soup 82
Boulangère potatoes 252

**bread**
Tomato & olive French toast 22–3

**broad beans** 9
Broad bean, radish and potato salad 40
Succotash 158
Summer vegetable soup 80

**broccoli** 9
Bean, marinated tofu & broccoli salad 44

Black bean & chipotle tacos 172
Chilli bean bake 156
Indian bubble & squeak 28
Sweet & sour tofu 132
Brownies, Dairy-free 242
**Brussels sprouts** 9
Brussels sprout & chestnut
barley risotto 124
**buckwheat flour**
Biker blinis 96
Burgers, Biker 196
**butter beans** 9
Succotash 158
**buttermilk**
Stuffed cornbread 170
**butternut squash** 9
Basic vegetable stock 276
Chilli bean bake 156
Indian shepherd's pie 186
Moroccan tomato soup 78
Pasta with creamy black pepper
sauce 134
Roast vegetable lasagne 178
Stuffed cornbread 170
Succotash 158
Vegan plate pie 148

**cabbage** 9
American-style layered salad 58
Caribbean-style vegetable soup
84
Indian bubble & squeak 28
Roast cabbage 258
Sautéed cabbage 257
*see also* Chinese cabbage
**cakes**
Lemon bundt cake 236
Orange polenta cake 234
Vegan Christmas cake 244–5
calcium 9
**cannellini beans** 9
Artichoke & fennel paella 204
Chilli bean bake 156

Pasta & bean soup 82
Caramelised endive 258
Caramelised onion, potato &
greens galette 182
Caribbean-style vegetable soup 84
**carrots** 9
American-style layered salad 58
Basic vegetable stock 276
Carrot & swede purée 256
Chickpea pancakes with spicy
carrot & bean curry 18
Chow mein 140
Indian shepherd's pie 186
Mushroom bourguignon cobbler
180
Ramen 74
Root vegetable tray bake 136
Tom yum soup 66
Vegan figgy pudding 228
Vegan plate pie 148
Vegetable biryani 184–5
Winter vegetable soup with
dumplings 64
**cashew nuts** 9
Coffee crème brûlée 218
Pasta with creamy black pepper
sauce 134
Quick jackfruit korma 146
Vegan cream sauce 262
**cauliflower** 9
Cauliflower rice 256
Cauliflower tikka masala 192
Masala frittata 16
Vegetable biryani 184–5
Roast cauliflower steaks 142
**celeriac**
Indian shepherd's pie 186
Jerusalem artichoke & celeriac
soup 72
Root vegetable purées 255
Root vegetable tray bake 136
Vegan plate pie 148
Winter vegetable soup with
dumplings 64
**celery**
Basic vegetable stock 276

Celery soup 70
Indian shepherd's pie 186
Pasta & bean soup 82
Winter vegetable soup with
dumplings 64
**chard**
Caramelised onion, potato &
greens galette 182
Indian bubble & squeak 28
Pasta & bean soup 82
Sautéed chard 257
**cheese, vegetarian** 10
Caramelised onion, potato &
greens galette 182
Cheese & Marmite scones 92
Cheese & tomato savoury
cakes 94
Cheese, potato & onion
pasties 116
Gnocchi with blue cheese sauce
190–91
Masala frittata 16
Mushroom bourguignon cobbler
180
Mushroom risotto 188
Stuffed baked potatoes 138
Stuffed cornbread 170
Stuffed crispy pancakes 166
Tomato & burrata salad 56
*see also* cream cheese; goat's
cheese; halloumi; mozzarella
Cherry compote 216
**chestnuts** 9
Brussels sprout & chestnut
barley risotto 124
Christmas veggie Wellington
206–7
**chickpea flour (gram)**
Chickpea pancakes with spicy
carrot & bean curry 18
Pickled onion bhajis 112
**chickpeas** 270
Cauliflower tikka masala 192
Chickpea garnish (for tagine)
154
Fab falafel 114

Gnocchi with blue cheese sauce 190–91

Moroccan tomato soup 78

Palak paneer & chickpeas 164

Red pepper humus 102

Roasted chickpeas 106

*see also* aquafaba

Chilli bean bake 156

**Chinese cabbage**

Chow mein 140

Potstickers 100

Ramen 74

Chipotle sauce 172

**chocolate**

Dairy-free brownies 242

Oatmeal chocolate chip cookies 240

Vegan chocolate mousse 214

Chow mein 140

Christmas cake, Vegan 244—5

Christmas veggie Wellington 206–7

Clafoutis, Apricot 230

cobbler

Mushroom bourguignon cobbler 180

Coconut ice cream with coconut salted caramel 220

**coconut milk**

Caribbean-style vegetable soup 84

Coconut ice cream with coconut salted caramel 220

Coconut rice 273

Keema peas with paneer 144

Rice & peas 273

Tempeh rendang 126

Tom yum soup 66

Vegan chocolate mousse 214

Coffee crème brûlée 218

**coriander**

Chickpea pancakes 18

Coriander rice 273

Coriander yoghurt sauce 16

Keema peas with paneer 144

Tom yum soup 66

Cornbread, Stuffed 170

**corn cobs**

Dirty corn 200–1

**cornmeal**

Cornbread batter 170

*see also* Orange polenta cake

**courgettes**

Couscous-stuffed peppers 128

Grilled vegetable & freekeh salad 50

Mediterranean-style vegetable bake 152

Pasta & bean soup 82

Roast vegetable lasagne 178

Stuffed pasta shells 194

Succotash 158

Summer vegetable soup 80

Vegan pizzas 198

**couscous**

Couscous salad 142

Couscous-stuffed peppers 128

Fennel & turnip tagine 154

Cranberry sauce 207

**cream cheese**

Artichoke & basil dip 102

Biker blinis 96

Crisps, Potato skin 107

**cucumber**

Greek salad with roast tomatoes & halloumi 48

Grilled vegetable & freekeh salad 50

Pickles 176

Turnip & cucumber pickles 46

**curries**

Aubergine katsu 176

Cauliflower tikka masala 192

Chickpea pancakes with spicy carrot & bean curry 18

Indian shepherd's pie 186

A quick dal 254

Quick jackfruit korma 146

*see also* Vegetable biryani

Custard, Vegan 264

Dal 254

Dauphinoise potatoes 251

Dave's special pretzels 110–11

**dips**

Artichoke & basil dip 102

Dill & yoghurt dip 90

Yoghurt & mango chutney dip 112

dipping sauce (for Potstickers) 100

Dirty corn 200–1

**dried fruit, mixed** 9

Spicy baked apples 226

Vegan Christmas cake 244–5

**Dumplings** 64

Chinese dumplings *see* Potstickers

# E

**edamame beans**

Bean, marinated tofu & broccoli salad 44

**eggs** 10

Asparagus mimosa 54

Banana tray bake 238

Batter 230

Farmhouse hash 26

Masala frittata 16

Tamago eggs 265

Tomato & olive French toast 22–3

Enchiladas, Veggie 202—3

Endive, Caramelised 258

# F

Fab falafel 114

Farmhouse hash 26

**fennel bulbs**

Artichoke & fennel paella 204

Fennel & turnip tagine 154

Fermented tomatoes 260

**figs** 9

Vegan figgy pudding 228

**freekeh**

Grilled vegetable & freekeh salad 50

Frittata, Masala 16

Fritters, Tomato 90

# G

**galette**

Caramelised onion, potato & greens galette 182

**garlic**

Cream of mushroom soup 76

Garlic sauce 104

Pasta & bean soup 82

Ramen 74

Veggie enchiladas 202–3

Gnocchi with blue cheese sauce 190–91

**goat's cheese**

Dirty corn 200–1

Leek & goat's cheese tart 168

Roast beetroot, goat's cheese & apple salad 36

gram *see* chickpea flour

Gravy 207

Greek salad with roast tomatoes & halloumi 48

**green bean**s 9

Artichoke & fennel paella 204

Chickpea pancakes with spicy carrot & bean curry 18

Green bean, orange & hazelnut salad 42

Indian shepherd's pie 186

Thai spiced mushroom salad 52

Guacamole 172

Gyoza wrappers 267

Potstickers 100

# H

**halloumi**

Greek salad with roast tomatoes & halloumi 48

**haricot beans** 9

Home-made baked beans 253

**Hazelnuts** 9

Green bean, orange & hazelnut salad 42

Hummus, Red pepper 102

# I

Indian bubble & squeak 28

Indian shepherd's pie 186

# J

**jackfruit**

Quick jackfruit korma 146

**jalapeños**

Stuffed cornbread 170

Tomato salsa 38

Veggie enchiladas 202–3

Jammy dodgers 232

**Jerusalem artichokes**

Jerusalem artichoke & celeriac soup 72

Root vegetable purées 255

# K

**kale** 9

Caramelised onion, potato & greens galette 182

Indian bubble & squeak 28

Noodle salad with greens & mushrooms 46

Pasta & bean soup 82

Sautéed kale 257

Winter vegetable soup with

dumplings 64

Katsu sauce 176

Keema peas with paneer 144

Key lime pie 222

**kidney beans** 9

Caribbean-style vegetable soup 84

Rice & peas 273

Veggie enchiladas 202–3

**kievs**

Mushroom mini kievs 174–5

**kombu**

Ramen 74

**korma**

Quick jackfruit korma 146

# L

**lamb's lettuce**

Roast beetroot, goat's cheese & apple salad 36

**lasagne**

Roast vegetable lasagne 178

**leeks**

Basic vegetable stock 276

Cream of mushroom soup 76

Leek & goat's cheese tart 168

Stuffed baked potatoes 138

Summer vegetable soup 80

Vegan plate pie 148

**lemons**

Artichoke & basil dip 102

Fennel & turnip tagine 154

Lemon bundt cake 236

Lemon rice 272

Paneer 144

salad dressings 40, 44, 50

**lentils** 9

Green bean, orange & hazelnut salad 42

Indian shepherd's pie 186

Keema peas with paneer 144

Moroccan tomato soup 78

Red lentil & herb soup 68

Vegan sausage rolls 98–9

**lettuce**
American-style layered salad 58
Greek salad with roast tomatoes
& halloumi 48
Mexican buddha bowl 38
Summer vegetable soup 80
**limes/lime juice**
Key lime pie 222
Lime-pickled red onion 38
Lime rice 272

# M

**Marmite**
Cheese & Marmite scones 92
Masala frittata 16
Masala potato topping 186
Mediterranean-style vegetable
bake 152
Meringue 224
Mexican buddha bowl 38
**milk, plant-based** 11
American-style pancakes 30
Celery soup 70
Dairy-free brownies 242
Pasta with creamy black pepper
sauce 134
Vegan custard 264
minerals 9
**miso paste**
Ramen 74
Moroccan tomato soup 78
**mousse**
Vegan chocolate mousse 214
mozzarella
Chilli bean bake 156
Roast vegetable lasagne 178
Tomato & olive French toast
22–3
*see also* Tomato & burrata salad
**mushrooms**
Chow mein 140
Cream of mushroom soup 76
Farmhouse hash 26

Gravy 207
Mushroom bourguignon cobbler
180
Mushroom duxelles 206
Mushroom mini kievs 174–5
Mushroom risotto 188
Mushroom stock 277
Noodle salad with greens &
mushrooms 46
Thai spiced mushroom salad 52
Tofu scramble fry up 20

# N

**noodles**
Chow mein 140
Noodle salad with greens &
mushrooms 46
Ramen 74
**nori sushi seaweed**
Ramen 74

# O

Oatmeal chocolate chip cookies
240
okra 9
Succotash 158
**onions** 10
Artichoke & fennel paella 204
Basic vegetable stock 276
Caramelised onion, potato &
greens galette 182
Cheese, potato & onion pasties
116
Indian shepherd's pie 186
Lime-pickled red onion 38
Moroccan tomato soup 78
Mushroom bourguignon cobbler
180
Pickled onion bhajis 112
Red lentil & herb soup 68
Roast vegetable lasagne 178
Root vegetable tray bake 136

Stuffed cornbread 170
Sweet & sour tofu 132
Vegan sausage rolls 98–9
Vegetable biryani 184–5
Veggie enchiladas 202–3
**oranges** 9
Cranberry sauce 207
Green bean, orange & hazelnut
salad 42
Orange polenta cake 234
Roast cauliflower steaks 142

# P

Padron pepper tempura 107
**paella**
Artichoke & fennel paella 204
**pak choi**
Tom yum soup 66
Palak paneer & chickpeas 164
**pancakes**
American-style pancakes 30
Chickpea pancakes with spicy
carrot & bean curry 18
Stuffed crispy pancakes 166
**Paneer** 144
Palak paneer & chickpeas 164
**parsnips**
Roast potatoes and parsnips
250
Root vegetable purées 255
Winter vegetable soup with
dumplings 64
**pasta**
Pasta & bean soup 82
Pasta with creamy black pepper
sauce 134
Roast vegetable lasagne 178
Roasted aubergine pasta 150
Spaghetti & 'meatballs' 130
Stuffed pasta shells 194
**pasties**
Cheese, potato & onion pasties
116

**pastry**
Shortcrust 268
Vegan pastry 268
**pavlova**
Summer berries pavlova 224
**peas** 9
Keema peas with paneer 144
Pea and mint pesto 80
Summer vegetable soup 80
**peppers**
Artichoke & fennel paella 204
Caribbean-style vegetable soup
84
Couscous-stuffed peppers 128
Indian shepherd's pie 186
Mediterranean-style vegetable
bake 152
Padron pepper tempura 107
Red pepper humus 102
Roast vegetable lasagne 178
Stuffed cornbread 170
Sweet & sour tofu 132
Veggie enchiladas 202–3
**pesto**
Pea and mint pesto 80
**pickles**
Lime-pickled red onion 38
Pickled onion bhajis 112
Radish pickles 176
Turnip & cucumber pickles 46
**pinto beans** 9
Veggie enchiladas 202–3
Pizzas, Vegan 198
potassium 9
**potatoes** 9
American-style layered salad 58
Boulangère potatoes 252
Broad bean, radish and potato
salad 40
Caramelised onion, potato &
greens galette 182
Cheese, potato & onion pasties
116
Dauphinoise potatoes 251
Farmhouse hash 26

Gnocchi with blue cheese sauce
190–91
Indian bubble & squeak 28
Indian shepherd's pie 186
Jerusalem artichoke & celeriac
soup 72
Masala frittata 16
Mediterranean-style vegetable
bake 152
Mushroom mini kievs 174–5
Potato skin crisps 107
Roast potatoes & parsnips 250
Root vegetable purées 255
Stuffed baked potatoes 138
Summer vegetable soup 80
Tattie scones 24
Tempeh rendang 126
Vegan pizzas 198
Winter vegetable soup with
dumplings 64
Potstickers 100
Pretzels, Dave's special 110–11
**prunes** 9
Armagnac soaked prunes 218
Christmas veggie Wellington
206–7
**pumpkin**
Basic vegetable stock 276
Caribbean-style vegetable soup
84
Chilli bean bake 156
Roast vegetable lasagne 178
Stuffed cornbread 170
Succotash 158
Vegan plate pie 148

# Q

Quick dal 254
Quick jackfruit korma 146
**quinoa** 271
Mexican buddha bowl 38
**Quorn mince**
Keema peas with paneer 144

# R

**radishes**
American-style layered salad 58
Broad bean, radish and potato
salad 40
Pickles 176
Raita 262
Ramen 74
**raspberries**
Summer berries pavlova 224
**redcurrants**
Summer berries pavlova 224
Red lentil & herb soup 68
Rendang, Tempeh 126
**rice** 272
Almond rice pudding & cherry
compote 216
Artichoke & fennel paella 204
Bean, marinated tofu & broccoli
salad 44
Coconut rice 273
Coriander rice 273
Lemon rice 273
Lime rice 273
Rice & peas 273
Thai-spiced mushroom salad 52
Vegetable biryani 184–5
*see also* risotti

**risotti** 11
Brussels sprout & chestnut
barley risotto 124
Mushroom risotto 188
**root vegetables, mixed**
Christmas veggie Wellington
206–7
Roast potatoes and parsnips
250
Root vegetable purées 255
Root vegetable tray bake 136
Winter vegetable soup with
dumplings 64

**runner beans**
Vegetable biryani 184–5

# S

Sage & onion balls 136
**salads**
American-style layered salad 58
Asparagus mimosa 54
Bean, marinated tofu & broccoli
salad 44
Broad bean, radish and potato
salad 40
Couscous salad 142
Greek salad with roast tomatoes
& halloumi 48
Green bean, orange & hazelnut
salad 42
Grilled vegetable & freekeh salad
50
Mexican buddha bowl 38
Noodle salad with greens &
mushrooms 46
Roast beetroot, goat's cheese &
apple salad 36
Thai-spiced mushroom salad 52
Tomato & burrata salad 56
Sandwiches, BLT (vegan style) 118
**sauces**
Barbecue sauce 200
Béchamel sauce 178
Blue cheese sauce 190, 191
Burger sauce 196
Chipotle sauce 172
Coriander yoghurt sauce 16
Cranberry sauce 207
Garlic sauce 104
Katsu sauce 176
Raita 262
Salted caramel sauce 220
Sweet & sour sauce 132
Tahini sauce 114
Tomato sauce 263
Vegan cream sauce 262

**'sausagemeat'/'sausages'**
Barbecue sauce and sausages
200
Farmhouse hash 26
Vegan sausage rolls 98–9
Sautéed greens 257
**scones**
Cheese & Marmite scones 92
Tattie scones 24
**shallots**
Thai spiced mushroom salad 52
Shawarma, Tempeh 104
Shepherd's pie, Indian 186
**soups**
Caribbean-style vegetable soup
84
Celery soup 70
Cream of mushroom soup 76
Jerusalem artichoke & celeriac
soup 72
Moroccan tomato soup 78
Pasta & bean soup 82
Ramen 74
Red lentil & herb soup 68
Summer vegetable soup 80
Tom yum soup 66
Winter vegetable soup with
dumplings 64
Spaghetti & 'meatballs' 130
Spice mix, Biker 266
Spicy baked apples 226
**spinach** 9
Broad bean, radish & potato
salad 40
Mushroom duxelles 206
Palak paneer & chickpeas 164
Pasta with creamy black pepper
sauce 134
Quick jackfruit korma 146
Stuffed crispy pancakes 166
Stuffed pasta shells 194
Tofu scramble fry-up 20
**spring greens**
Indian bubble & squeak 28
Pasta & bean soup 82

Sautéed greens 257
**spring onions**
Chow mein 140
Ramen 74
Tom yum soup 66
sprouts *see* Brussels sprouts
squash *see* butternut squash
**stocks** 11
Basic vegetable stock 276
Mushroom stock 277
**strawberries**
Summer berries pavlova 224
Stuffed baked potatoes 138
Stuffed cornbread 170
Stuffed crispy pancakes 166
Stuffed pasta shells 194
Succotash 158
Summer berries pavlova 224
Summer vegetable soup 80
**swede**
Winter vegetable soup with
dumplings 64
Sweet & sour tofu 132
**sweetcorn**
Mexican buddha bowl 38
Roasted sweetcorn 38
Stuffed cornbread 170
Succotash 158
**sweet potatoes**
Caribbean-style vegetable soup
84
Root vegetable purées 255
Vegan plate pie 148

# T

**tacos**
Black bean & chipotle tacos 172
**tagine**
Fennel & turnip tagine 154
**tagliatelle**
Pasta with creamy black pepper
sauce 134
Tahini sauce 114

**Tamago eggs** 265
    Ramen 74
Tamari almonds 106
**tarts**
    Caramelised onion, potato &
        greens galette 182
    Leek & goat's cheese tart 168
Tattie scones 24
Tempeh rendang 126
Tempeh shawarma 104
Tempura, Padron pepper 107
Thai-spiced mushroom salad 52
**tofu**
    Bean, marinated tofu & broccoli
        salad 44
    Key lime pie 222
    Sweet & sour tofu 132
    Tom yum soup 66
    *see also* Keema peas with
        paneer; Ramen; tofu bacon
**tofu bacon** 266
    American-style layered salad 58
    BLT sandwiches, vegan style
        118, 266
    Tofu scramble fry up 20, 266
Tom yum soup 66
**tomatoes**
    American-style layered salad 58
    Cauliflower tikka masala 192
    Cheese & tomato savoury cakes
        94
    Chilli bean bake 156
    Fermented tomatoes 260
    Greek salad with roast tomatoes
        & halloumi 48
    Grilled vegetable & freekeh salad
        50
    Home-made baked beans 253
    Keema peas with paneer 144
    Mediterranean style vegetable
        bake 152
    Mexican buddha bowl 38
    Moroccan tomato soup 78
    Quick tomato relish 259
    Roasted aubergine pasta 150

Succotash 158
Tofu scramble fry up 20
Tom yum soup 66
Tomato & burrata salad 56
Tomato & olive French toast
    22–3
Tomato fritters 90
Tomato salsa 38
Tomato sauce 263
**tortillas**
    Black bean & chipotle tacos 172
    Veggie enchiladas 202–3
**tray bakes**
    Banana tray bake 238
    Root vegetable tray bake 136
**turnips**
    Fennel & turnip tagine 154
    Turnip & cucumber pickles 46
    Winter vegetable soup with
        dumplings 64

# V

**vegetables, mixed**
    Basic vegetable stock 276
    Mediterranean-style vegetable
        bake 152
    Roast vegetable lasagne 178
    Succotash 158
    Vegan plate pie 148
    Vegetable biryani 184–5
    *see also* root vegetables; salads
Veggie enchiladas 202–3
vitamins 9

# W

Whisky cream 226
Winter vegetable soup with
    dumplings 64

# Y

**yoghurt**
    Chipotle sauce 172
    Coriander yoghurt sauce 16
    Dill & yoghurt dip 90
    Garlic sauce 104
    Raita 262
    Yoghurt & mango chutney dip
        112
    Yoghurt dressing 164

# Z

zinc 9

# Biggest thank you ever

Our always wonderful team have really surpassed themselves this time and together we've come up with what we think is our best book.

Catherine Phipps, worker of culinary magic, has helped us turn our wild ideas to recipe gold and made our veggie visions come true, while Andrew Hayes-Watkins and Suki Hayes-Watkins have worked together to bring us the most beautiful and tempting food photographs. They've gone beyond all expectations and we are so thrilled. Genius all of you, and we know you have worked your socks off for this. Big thanks to Lucie Stericker for the elegant design and art direction, and to Jinny Johnson for holding our hands throughout.

Thanks to Tamzin Ferdinando for finding the props for the pictures, to Elise See Tai for proofreading and Vicki Robinson for the index.

To Vicky Eribo and Anna Valentine at Orion – thanks for all your enthusiasm and support. It's great to have you both on the team. And thanks to Virginia Woolstencroft, head of publicity, for her input.

Huge love and thanks to Amanda Harris and our team at YMU: Emily Arthur, Natalie Zietcer, Louisa Barnard, Blaise McGowan, Demi Mantell, Olivia Bertolotti, Maryam Hamizadeh and Mary Bekhait.

We started working on this book back in January and then … Covid-19 struck!
But thanks to our amazing team – Andrew, Catherine, Jinny, Lucie and Suki – who worked
throughout safely, but in the most difficult and challenging circumstances, it all happened and we
are so very proud of what we've produced. We'd like to dedicate this book to you all with our love,
thanks and respect.

First published in Great Britain in 2020 by Seven Dials
an imprint of The Orion Publishing Group Ltd
Carmelite House, 50 Victoria Embankment
London EC4Y 0DZ

An Hachette UK Company

3 5 7 9 10 8 6 4 2

ISBN (Hardback) 978 1 8418 8429 5
ISBN (eBook) 978 1 8418 8430 1

Publisher: Vicky Eribo
Recipe consultant: Catherine Phipps
Photography and styling: Andrew Hayes-Watkins
Food stylist: Suki Hayes-Watkins
Design: Lucie Stericker
Editor: Jinny Johnson
Prop stylist: Tamzin Ferdinando
Proofreader: Elise See Tai
Indexer: Vicki Robinson
Production manager: Katie Horrocks

Printed in Germany

www.orionbooks.co.uk

For more delicious recipes plus exclusive competitions and sneak previews from Orion's cookery writers,
visit kitchentales.co.uk